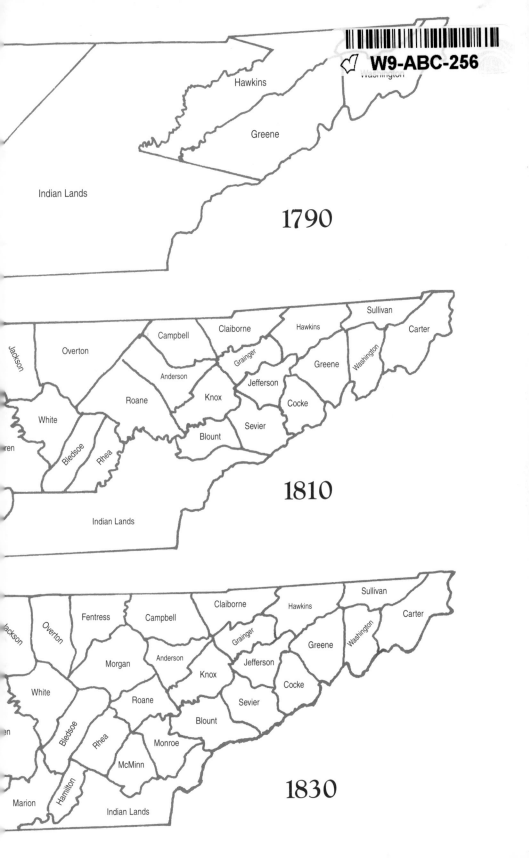

W9-ABC-256

Hawkins

Greene

Washington

Indian Lands

1790

Jackson

Overton

Campbell

Claiborne

Hawkins

Sullivan

Carter

Grainger

Greene

Washington

Anderson

Jefferson

Roane

Knox

Cocke

White

Sevier

Bledsoe

Rhea

Blount

ren

Indian Lands

1810

ackson

Overton

Fentress

Campbell

Claiborne

Hawkins

Sullivan

Carter

Grainger

Greene

Washington

Morgan

Anderson

Jefferson

White

Knox

Cocke

Roane

Sevier

Bledsoe

Rhea

Blount

en

Monroe

Hamilton

McMinn

Marion

Indian Lands

1830

TENNESSEE TAPROOTS

Other books by Sophie and Paul Crane

Korean Patterns—Paul Crane (1967, 4th edition 1978)

Tennessee's Troubled Roots: County Jails of Tennessee (1979)

North Carolina Taproots (forthcoming)

TENNESSEE TAPROOTS

COURTHOUSES OF TENNESSEE

REVISED EDITION

SOPHIE AND PAUL CRANE

HILLSBORO PRESS
Franklin, Tennessee

TENNESSEE HERITAGE LIBRARY
Bicentennial Collection

Copyright 1976, 1996 by Sophie and Paul Crane

All rights reserved. Written permission must be secured from the publisher to use or reproduce any part of this book, except for brief quotations in critical reviews or articles.

First edition 1976
Second edition 1996

Printed in the United States of America

02   01   00   99   98   97   6   5   4   3   2   1

Library of Congress Catalog Card Number: 96-75691

ISBN: 1-881576-26-4

Cover by Bozeman Design

Cover photo—Smith County Courthouse

Endsheet maps are from the Map Guide to the U.S. Federal Censuses, 1790–1920 *and used by permission.*

HILLSBORO PRESS
an imprint of
PROVIDENCE HOUSE PUBLISHERS
238 Seaboard Lane • Franklin, Tennessee 37067
800-321-5692

TO the Tennessee Bicentennial Celebration and to our grandchildren:

Brian Gleser
Eugene Gleser
Saul Gleser
Audrey Gleser
Rosie Gleser
Olivia Gleser
Luke Rainey
Benjamin Rainey
Andrew Rainey
Nathan Adams
Joshua Adams
Isaac Adams
David Crane
Marie Crane
Banks Crane

Preface to the Bicentennial Edition

Twenty years have passed since the first edition of TENNESSEE TAPROOTS appeared and promptly sold out; it has joined the list of rare books about Tennessee. Because of numerous requests for TENNESSEE TAPROOTS and because of the pleasure we experienced in touring the state to see and collect information, we decided to write an updated edition in honor of Tennessee's bicentennial.

We have revisited each of the ninety-five counties plus the "lost county of James" and, with a new state-of-the-art camera (8008 Nikon), rephotographed the courthouses. We have been amazed to find how Tennessee has grown during the past two decades in population, industries, and general activity. Many of the courthouses have been renovated, added to, or generally spruced up as if waiting for us to come by to take their pictures once again. We have corrected errors in the first edition, added new facts of history, population figures, per capita income, ethnic breakdown, parks, and persons of note.

We hope this book will be a useful guide to a wonderful and beautiful area, and to the rich heritage and delightful people that make up the Volunteer State.

Tennessee County Historians (1995)

State Historian—Mrs. Wilma Dykeman Stokely

County	Historian	County	Historian
Anderson	Ms. Sue Harris	Johnson	Mr. Thomas W. Gentry
Bedford	Mr. Richard Poplin	Knox	Mrs. Park Niceley
Benton	Mrs. Virginia L. Whitworth	Lake	Ms. Abigail Hyde
Bledsoe	Miss Elizabeth Robnett	Lauderdale	Mr. Terry Ford
Blount	Mrs. Inez Burns	Lawrence	Mrs. Kathy Niedergeses
Bradley	Dr. Bill Snell	Lewis	Ms. Marjorie B. Graves
Campbell	None	Lincoln	Mrs. Sarah B. Posey
Cannon	Mr. Harold Patrick	Loudon	Mr. Joe Spence
Carroll	Mrs. Mary Ruth Devault	Macon	Mr. Harold Blankenship
Carter	None	Madison	Mr. Harbert Alexander
Cheatham	Mr. James B. Hallums	Marion	Mrs. Patsy Beene
Chester	Mr. Bobby Barnes	Marshall	Ms. Charlene Nicholas
	Mr. Lewis Jones	Maury	Mrs. Marise Lightfoot
	Mr. James Williams	McMinn	Mr. Bill Akins
Claiborne	Mr. John J. Kivette	McNairy	Mr. Bill Wagoner
Clay	Mrs. W. B. Upton	Meigs	Ms. Shirley Jennings
Cocke	Mr. Edward R. Walker III		Ms. Paulette Jones
Coffee	Mr. Jess Lewis Jr.	Monroe	Mr. Walter Lumsden Jr.
Crockett	Mrs. Charles C. James	Montgomery	Ms. Eleanor Williams
Cumberland	Mr. Donald Brookhart	Moore	Mrs. Joyce Neal
Davidson	Mr. John L. Connelly	Morgan	Mr. Donald Todd
Decatur	Mrs. Lillye Younger	Obion	Mr. Rebel C. Forrester
DeKalb	Mr. Thomas G. Webb	Overton	None
Dickson	Mr. George Jackson	Perry	Mr. Gus A. Steele
Dyer	Mr. Wallace Milan	Pickett	Mr. Richard W. Pierce
Fayette	Mrs. J. R. Morton	Polk	Ms. Marian Presswood
Fentress	Ms. Lorraine Cargile	Putnam	Ms. Pat Franklin
Franklin	Mr. Howard M. Hannah	Rhea	Ms. Betty Broyles
Gibson	Mr. Fred Culp	Roane	Mr. J. C. Parker
Giles	Mrs. Pauline Cross	Robertson	Ms. Yolanda Reid
Grainger	Mr. John M. Clark	Rutherford	Mr. Ernest K. Johns
Greene	Mr. T. Elmer Cox	Scott	Ms. Irene Baker
Grundy	Ms. Margaret Coppinger	Sequatchie	Mr. Henry Camp
	Mr. William Ray Turner	Sevier	Mrs. Beulah D. Linn
Hamblen	Mrs. Berwin Haun	Shelby	Mr. Edward F. Williams III
Hamilton	Mr. John Wilson	Smith	Mr. Ervin Smith
Hancock	Mr. Scott Collins	Stewart	Ms. Nelda Saunders
Hardeman	Mrs. Faye Tennyson Davidson	Sullivan	Dr. Elery A. Lay
Hardin	Ms. Mary Hitchcock	Sumner	Dr. John Garrett
Hawkins	Mr. Henry R. Price	Tipton	Mr. Russell Bailey
Haywood	Ms. Lynn Shaw	Trousdale	Mr. Web Ross
	Mrs. J. C. Nunn	Unicoi	Mr. Walter B. Garland
	Mr. Ray Dixon	Union	Ms. Bonnie H. Peters
Henderson	Mr. Randy Hart	Van Buren	Mr. Earl J. Madewell
Henry	Ms. Mary Ashley Morris	Warren	Mr. James A. Dillon Jr.
Hickman	Mr. Edward Dotson	Washington	Mrs. Ruth Broyles
Houston	Mr. George Bateman	Wayne	Mr. Alf Scott
Humphreys	Mrs. Bill Anderson	Weakley	Mrs. Virginia C. Vaughan
	Mr. John H. Whitfield	White	Ms. Mary West
Jackson	Ms. Moldon Tayse	Williamson	Mrs. Joe Bowman
Jefferson	Dr. E. P. Muncy	Wilson	Mr. William Simms

Introduction

TENNESSEE TAPROOTS is a book of discovery—our discovery of Tennessee through its county courthouses. As new residents of the state, we began to notice the many interesting courthouses, no two of which are alike. In the process of photographing them, we became collectors. So fascinated did we become that we journeyed to all ninety-five counties (plus the "lost" county of James) for a complete set of pictures of the courthouses. We came to realize that the county courthouse is an icon, a symbol of the county, often accurately reflecting the economic activity, civic pride, and health of local government. The county courthouse system is a basic building block of democracy in America and is still the "temple of justice" where the ordinary citizen meets his or her government, the very taproots of Tennessee.

The courthouse is the repository of records: genealogies, births and deaths, marriages and divorces, wills, civil and criminal cases tried, and, especially, land dealings carefully recorded in great ledgers. All citizens are free to inspect the courthouse records. This intensely personal encounter of the citizens and their government is part of what makes the courthouse important in our society.

The courthouse often becomes the focal point of social activity in the county seat (political rallies, Fourth of July celebrations, the Jonesborough Day in Washington County, the Bluegrass Festival in DeKalb County). War monuments pay tribute to the heroes of the county. Monuments and statues of local celebrities abound. The ninety-five courthouses of Tennessee are shown as they appeared in 1995.

Three types of information are presented. The first is the factual information about the county which, although available in the public domain, has not been brought together in one volume. The second type of information has to do specifically with the courthouse itself. The third lists some of the folklore, items of interest, significant happenings, governors, and famous personalities.

A list, showing construction dates, portrays an interesting architectural history of the courthouses and the ever-changing styles. As with vintage wine, there are the good decades and the not-so-good decades for building courthouses. Fortunately for Tennessee, the good years outnumber the poorer ones. It is probable that some of the modern functional buildings are, for those who labor in them, more comfortable than the courthouses whose appeal is more to the artistic eye.

The first county established in Tennessee was Washington County in 1777 with Jonesborough as the county seat. The youngest counties are Pickett and Chester both established in 1879. The name of Wisdom County was changed to Chester County, and James County was dissolved in 1920. The largest county, both in land area and population, is Shelby (Memphis); smallest in population is Pickett (Byrdstown); smallest in land area, Trousdale (Hartsville).

Population trends show that while some counties are growing rapidly (such as Williamson County), some are declining or showing little growth (such as Lake County). The ethnic mix of African Americans, Native Americans, Asians, Hispanics, and Whites varies greatly from county to county. The per capita income varies from a low of 51 percent of the national average (Hancock and Van Buren Counties) to 131 percent of the national average (Williamson County).

Only seven courthouses built before the Civil War are in use today: Dickson County (Charlotte), Haywood County (Brownsville) Hawkins County (Rogersville), Jefferson County (Dandridge), Carter County, (Elizabethton), Rutherford County, (Murfreesboro) and Williamson County (Franklin).

Fire seems to be the great enemy of courthouses. Two courthouses (Marion and Grundy Counties) have burned since the first edition of Tennessee Taproots. There would appear to be at times a relation between the scheduled audits of the county books and the sudden outbreak of fires that have destroyed at least eighty-two of Tennessee's courthouses.

Tennessee, named the "Volunteer State" during the War of 1812 when some counties sent more men to the war than they had registered voters, has produced a fair share of great names in American history. National figures have often come from small rural Tennessee counties. Familiar names to most Americans are Andrew Jackson, James Knox Polk, Andrew Johnson, Cordell Hull, David

Crockett, Sam Davis, Admiral David G. Farragut, Nathan Bedford Forrest, William C. Handy, Sam Houston, Nancy Ward, Alvin C. York, Casey Jones, Alex Haley, Buford Pusser, Howard Baker, Lamar Alexander, Vice President Al Gore, and world famous entertainers such as Eddie Arnold, Elvis Presley, Chet Atkins, the late "King of Country Music" Roy Acuff, the late Minnie Pearl, Dolly Parton, Barbara Mandrell, and, of course, Johnny Cash.

We owe a major debt to the county historians who responded generously to our requests for help. The late Robert M. McBride, gifted editor of the *Tennessee Historical Quarterly*, encouraged us with his comments and advice. We would also like to thank the following: Herbert L. Harper, Claudette Stager, and Elizabeth Straw of the Tennessee Historical Commission; Jim Summerville, Mary Glenn Hearne of the Nashville Room of the Ben West Public Library; and the staffs of the Tennessee State Library and Archives and the Old Hickory Library. Our special thanks to Mr. Reuben M. Gulbenk for suggesting the name "Tennessee Taproots" and to Mr. Rob R. Schmid for suggesting that the end sheet maps show the historical development of the counties. We assume responsibility for errors made and stand ready to learn and be corrected.

As one travels to the four corners of the state, from the high country of Johnson County in the northeast, to the bluffs of Memphis in Shelby County on the great Mississippi River, or from the copper barrens of Polk County in the southeast to Lake County in the northwest, one cannot help but be impressed with the diversity, the beauty, the forests, the mountains, the hidden valleys, the rivers, the lakes, the waterfalls, the mineral springs, the caves, the farms, the proud horses, the great industries, and the people (all 4,877,185 plus) that make up the state of Tennessee. In our travels, we have found that Tennesseans have kept the open frontier cordiality that accepts people at face value and look to the future rather than probing the past.

We hope that TENNESSEE TAPROOTS will be a pleasant companion for those who enjoy discovering Tennessee.

Tennessee County Courthouses—Architectural Chronology

1833	Dickson County, Charlotte		1925	Fayette County, Somerville
1836	Hawkins County, Rogersville		1925	Marion County, Jasper
1844	Haywood County, Brownsville		1926	Campbell County, Jacksboro
1845	Jefferson County, Dandridge		1926	Hickman County, Centerville
1852	Carter County, Elizabethton		1927	Jackson County, Gainesboro
1859	Rutherford County, Murfreesboro		1928	Decatur County, Decaturville
1859	Williamson County, Franklin		1928	Perry County, Linden
1868	Hardeman County, Bolivar		1929	Marshall County, Lewisburg
1869	Overton County, Livingston		1930	Cocke County, Newport
1871	Coffee County, Manchester		1931	Carroll County, Huntingdon
1871	Crockett County, Alamo		1931	Hancock County, Sneedville
1872	Clay County, Celina		1933	Claiborne County, Tazewell
1872	Loudon County, Loudon		1933	Macon County, Lafayette
1874	Hamblen County, Morristown		1935	Bedford County, Shelbyville
1875	Smith County, Carthage		1935	Pickett County, Byrdstown
1878	Montgomery County, Clarksville		1936	Cannon County, Woodbury
1879	Robertson County, Springfield		1936	Lauderdale County, Ripley
1885	Knox County, Knoxville		1936	Madison County, Jackson
1885	Moore County, Lynchburg		1937	Davidson County, Nashville
1889	Tipton County, Covington		1937	Franklin County, Winchester
1891	Rhea County, Dayton		1937	Polk County, Benton
1896	Henry County, Paris		1939	Lewis County, Hohenwald
1896	Sevier County, Sevierville		1939	Obion County, Union City
1897	Monroe County, Madisonville		1940	Sumner County, Gallatin
1897	Warren County, McMinnville		1948	McNairy County, Selmer
1900	Putnam County, Cookeville		1948	Scott County, Huntsville
1901	Gibson County, Trenton		1949	Grainger County, Rutledge
1904	Lake County, Tiptonville		1950	Weakley County, Dresden
1904	Meigs County, Decatur		1952	Hardin County, Savannah
1904	Morgan County, Wartburg		1952	Humphreys County, Waverly
1905	Cumberland County, Crossville		1957	Houston County, Erin
1905	Trousdale County, Hartsville		1958	Johnson County, Mountain City
1906	Fentress County, Jamestown		1961	Henderson County, Lexington
1906	Maury County, Columbia		1964	Bradley County, Cleveland
1906	Van Buren County, Spencer		1965	Stewart County, Dover
1907	Blount County, Maryville		1966	Wilson County, Lebanon
1909	Giles County, Pulaski		1967	Anderson County, Clinton
1909	Shelby County, Memphis		1967	McMinn County, Athens
1910	Bledsoe County, Pikeville		1971	DeKalb County, Smithville
1911	Dyer County, Dyersburg		1972	Lincoln County, Fayetteville
1911	Sequatchie County, Dunlap		1974	Benton County, Camden
1913	Chester County, Henderson		1974	Lawrence County, Lawrenceburg
1913	Hamilton County, Chattanooga		1974	Union County, Maynardsville
1913	James County, Ooltewah (lost county)		1975	Roane County, Kingston
1913	Washington County, Jonesborough		1975	Wayne County, Waynesboro
1914	Cheatham County, Ashland City		1975	White County, Sparta
1916	Greene County, Greeneville		1976	Unicoi County, Erwin
1920	Sullivan County, Blountville		1995	Grundy County, Altamont

TENNESSEE TAPROOTS

Anderson County was established in 1801; named in honor of U.S. Senator Joseph Anderson, judge of the territory south of the Ohio River. The county seat was named Burrville in honor of Aaron Burr until 1809 when the named was changed to Clinton in honor of either (historians differ) DeWitt Clinton or his uncle George Clinton both New York politicians.

The first court in Anderson County met in 1801 in the log residence of Joseph Denham in Eagle Bend. The second courthouse, a two-story rough stone structure with an outside stairway and log jail at the rear, was finished about 1830. The third courthouse, said to be the second finest in Tennessee, was built in 1889–1890 for $35,380. The present courthouse was completed in 1967 at a cost of $1,500,000. The architect was Martin J. Lide of Birmingham; builder, Davis Brothers. The Slover Memorial Chimes on top of the courthouse were given by his son in honor of H. Clay Slover, a prominent citizen of Anderson County.

The chimes, installed in 1937, are tied to an electric Westminster tower-clock and play the celebrated "Cambridge Quarters" each quarter hour. The eleven bells, weighing from 275 to 2000 pounds each, are Meneely bells of which there are few sets in the world.

Census: 1850—6,938 (Whites 6,391; Free Blacks 41; Slaves 506); **1950**—59,407; **1990**—68,250 (Whites 64,615; African Americans 2,763; Native Americans 243; Asians 547; Hispanics 381)

Per capita income (1991): $16,998; 89 percent of national average

Land area: 338 square miles; drained by the Clinch and Powell Rivers

Of interest: American Museum of Atomic Energy at Oak Ridge; Museum of Appalachia at Norris; Norris Dam State Resort Park, 2,400 acres; Oak Ridge Atomic Energy Area.

***Bedford County,*** established in 1807, was named for Revolutionary War officer Thomas Bedford Jr. Historians believe that Shelbyville was named for Evan Shelby, the father of Colonel Isaac Shelby (see Shelby County).

The first courthouse was built of logs around 1810. A brick courthouse, constructed in 1811, was destroyed by a tornado in 1830; rebuilt, it burned in 1863. The fourth courthouse, built in 1873, was burned in 1934 by a lynch mob angered by the escape of their intended victim. The present courthouse duplicated, as far as possible, the style of the 1873 building and was completed in 1935. Marr & Holman were the architects; Foster & Creighton Company, contractors. It was possible to salvage enough hand-made bricks to face the new building.

The Shelbyville Courthouse Square Historic District is on the National Register of Historic Places.

Census: 1850—21,511 (Whites 15,937; Free Blacks 72; Slaves 5,502); **1950**—22,627; **1990**—30,411 (Whites 27,097; African Americans 3,068; Native Americans 36; Asians 147; Hispanics 172)

Per capita income (1991): $14,923; 78 percent of national average

Land area: 474 square miles; drained by the Duck River

Of interest: The Tennessee Walking Horse National Celebration; Webb School at Bell Buckle. Governor Prentice Cooper (1895–1969), Democrat, served three terms from 1939 to 1945.

Benton County was established

January 1, 1836. Originally named in honor of Thomas Hart Benton, an antebellum politician who, in time, lost his popularity. In 1852 the county decided to change the honoree to David Benton, an early settler and veteran of the War of 1812.

There have been six courthouses in Benton County. The first courthouse, built of logs in 1836 at Tranquility near Camden, cost $22.50, measured 18 by 27 feet, and had a single door whose big cracks served as the only source of light. The second (1837–1854) was a two-story brick building constructed by Samuel Ingram for $3,270.18. The third (1855–1877), a two-story brick building, cost $5,998.75. The fourth courthouse (1877–1915) was a two-story brick building with a cupola. The fifth (1915–1972) was a large brick building. The present courthouse, completed in 1974, cost $500,000. The architects were Hart, Freeland and Roberts of Nashville; the contractor, Hugh Ward of Humboldt.

Census: 1850—6,315 (Whites 5,931; Free Blacks 21; Slaves 363); **1950**—11,495; **1990**—14,524 (Whites 14,109; African Americans 345; Native Americans 23; Asians 31; Hispanics 72)

Per capita income (1991): $13,659; 71 percent of national average

Land area: 394 square miles; eastern boundary is the Tennessee River

Of interest: Nathan Bedford Forrest State Historical Area, 840 acres; Natchez Trace State Resort Park, 42,000 acres (also in Carroll and Henderson Counties). Governor Thomas Clarke Rye (1863–1953), Democrat, served 1915–1919.

Benton County Seat—Camden, Tennessee 38320

Bledsoe County was established in 1807; named for Anthony Bledsoe, a captain in the Colonial Army of Virginia, major in the Revolutionary War, and colonel in the Tennessee Militia. One of the first settlers of Sumner County, he was killed near his home by Indians in 1789.

The first county seat was at Old Madison where a log courthouse, jail, and stocks were built. In 1815 the county seat moved to Pikeville and is named for Zebulon Montgomery Pike, the soldier-explorer for whom Pike's Peak in Colorado is also named.

The present courthouse was built in 1910 replacing one which burned in 1909. W. K. Brown was the architect and builder. Extensive renovations, including a new roof, were completed in 1982. The courthouse is on the National Register of Historic Places.

Census: 1850—5,959 (Whites 5,036; Free Blacks 96; Slaves 827); **1950**—8,561; **1990**—9,669 (Whites 9,242; African Americans 375; Native Americans 42; Asians 3; Hispanics 38)

Per capita income (1991): $10,718; 56 percent of national average

Land area: 406 square miles; drained by the Sequatchie River

Of interest: Bledsoe State Forest; Fall Creek Falls State Resort Park, 16,000 acres (also in Van Buren County). Governor James Beriah Frazier (1856–1937), Democrat, served 1903–1905.

Blount County was established in 1795; named in honor of William Blount, a member of the Continental Congress, governor of the territory south of the River Ohio, and governor of Tennessee. Maryville was named for his wife Mary Grainger Blount.

The first temporary courthouse was built in 1796. The second courthouse was a wooden structure built in 1804 at a cost of $571.33; Josiah Danforth, contractor. The third courthouse (1840) burned in 1879. The fourth courthouse, built in 1879 by J. F. Bauman at a total cost of $12,779.01, burned in 1906. The 1907 courthouse, relocated on the homesite of Dr. John W. Cates, cost $80,000 including furnishings. Bauman Brothers, were the architects; Brimer & England, contractors. The jail annex (1957) was built for $300,000. A second annex (1975) cost $1,900,000, with major courthouse restoration, in 1978.

Census: 1850—12,424 (Whites 11,213; Free Blacks 127; Slaves 1,084); **1950**—54,691; **1990**—85,969 (Whites 82,503; African Americans 2,783; Native American 195; Asians 409; Hispanics 368)

Per capita income (1991): $15,587; 81 percent of national average

Land area: 559 square miles; drained by the Holston and Little Tennessee Rivers

Of interest: The Alcoa Aluminum works; Great Smoky Mountains National Park; Maryville College; Tucka Leechee Caverns. Governor Sam Houston (1793–1863), Democrat, served 1827–1829; Governor Lamar Alexander (1940–), Republican, served 1979–1987.

 **Bradley County** was established in 1836; named for Colonel Edward Bradley of Shelby County who was colonel of the 15th Regiment of the Tennessee Volunteers (Bradley's) in the War of 1812. The county seat was named for the Revolutionary hero Colonel Benjamin Cleveland of North Carolina.

There have been four court-houses. The first of logs, built in 1836, was replaced in 1840 by a brick building costing $8000 with jail. The third courthouse was built in 1892 for $75,000. Hunt and Lamm were the architects. The present court-house was built in 1964. Selmon T. Franklin & Associates were the architects. The old post office now serves as an annex to the court-house. Bradley County was the last home of Chief John Ross before the Cherokee Nation was forced in 1838 to move to Oklahoma on the "Trail of Tears." The Red Clay State Historical Area is the site of the last eastern capital of the Cherokee Nation.

Census: 1850—12,259 (Whites 11,478; Free Blacks 37; Slaves 744); 1950—32,338; 1990—73,712 (Whites 70,132; African Americans 2,900; Native Americans 200; Asians 232; Hispanics 712)

Per capita income (1991): $15,260; 80 percent of national average

Land area: 329 square miles; drained by the Hiwassee River & tributaries

Of interest: Lee College; Ocoee Lake and hydroelectric project.

Campbell County was established in 1806; named for Colonel Arthur Campbell, veteran of the Revolutionary War, commander of the 70th Regiment of the Virginia Militia, and commissioner for the negotiation of the Indian Treaties of 1781. Jacksboro was named for Revolutionary War veteran, Captain John T. Jack.

Tradition holds that the first meeting of the court was held in a farm wagon. The first courthouse was built of stone in 1808–1809, but later it became a store. The second courthouse, built in 1855, burned in 1884. The third courthouse, a "handsome" and quite substantial brick building, was built in 1884. An annex was added to that brick structure in 1912. The present courthouse was built in 1926. A new wing was added in 1964; the jail is attached to the rear.

Census: 1850—6,068 (Whites 5,651; Free Blacks 99; Slaves 318); **1950**—34,369; **1990**—35,079 (Whites 34,727; African Americans 130; Native Americans 175; Asians 41; Hispanics 117)

Per capita income (1984): $11,663; 61 percent of the national average

Land area: 480 square miles; drained by the Clinch River and tributaries of the Cumberland River

Of interest: Cove Lake State Park, 1500 acres; Cumberland State Scenic Trail; Indian Mountain State Park; Norris Lake Dam State Park, 2,321 acres.

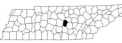

Cannon County was established

in 1836; named for Newton Cannon, veteran of the Creek War and the War of 1812, governor of Tennessee from 1835–1839, and U.S. congressman 1814–1817 and 1821–1827. Originally named Danville, the name of the county seat was changed to Woodbury in honor of General Levi Woodbury.

The first court was held in a tavern. The courthouse, built in 1836 by William Bates at a cost of $13,000, was washed away in the "freshet" of 1850. Bates added a spread eagle of gold leaf to the cupola. When the county commissioners refused to pay for the eagle while ruling that, since it was attached to the building, it could not legally be removed, Bates climbed to the top of the cupola early one morning, crowed like a rooster, and removed his golden eagle. A second courthouse built in 1852 was replaced in 1880 by a two-story brick building that burned in 1934. The present courthouse was completed in 1936 for $45,000 and is on the National Register of Historic Places. George D. Waller was the architect; Bell Brothers, the contractor.

Census: 1850—8,982 (Whites 8,115; Free Blacks 24; Slaves 843); **1950**—9,174; **1990**—10,467 (Whites 10,236; African Americans 186; Native Americans 15; Asians 14; Hispanics 39)

Per capita income (1991): $13,664; 71 percent of national average

Land area: 266 square miles; drained by numerous small streams

Of interest: In 1839, while on the "Trail of Tears" westward, 15,000 Cherokees camped for a time at Beaverdam and east of Hill Creek.

Carroll County was established in 1821 after Andrew Jackson and Isaac Shelby made a treaty with the Chickasaw Indians whereby all lands east of the Mississippi River were ceded to the United States; named for William Carroll, governor of Tennessee 1821–1827. Huntingdon was named for Mennican Hunt, Revolutionary War veteran.

There have been five courthouses in Carroll County. The first log courthouse was built without a floor and without a doorway "so that the worshipful Chairman of the Court [Nathan Nesbitt] brought his saw six miles from home to cut his way into the temple of justice." The second frame courthouse, measuring 20 by 24 feet, was built in 1824 and lasted until 1830. The 1830 courthouse was used until 1844. The fourth courthouse, a brick building costing $12,000, was built by Joel R. Smith and Thomas Banks, enlarged in 1897, and burned in 1931. The brick was subcontracted for one cent per brick. The present courthouse, modeled after the Lincoln Memorial, was built in 1931 for $100,000. Hart, Freeland and Roberts of Nashville were the architects; Chambers and Hightower, the contractors. Extensive renovation was carried out in 1981 by Barger Construction Co.

Census: 1850—15,967 (Whites 12,815; Free Blacks 17; Slaves 3,135); **1950**—26,553; **1990**—27,514 (Whites 24,303; African Americans 3,138; Native Americans 35; Asians 10; Hispanics 125)

Per capita income (1991): $13,318; 69 percent of national average

Land area: 599 square miles; drained by Big Sandy and Obion Rivers

Of interest: Bethel College; Natchez Trace State Resort Park, 42,000 acres (also in Henderson and Benton Counties). Governor Alvin Hawkins (1821–1905), Republican, served 1881–1883; Governor Gordon Browning (1889–1976), Democrat, served 1937–1939 and 1949–1953.

Carter County was established by the General Assembly of Tennessee in April 1796 before the state was admitted to the Union June 1, 1796; named for Landon Carter, speaker of the first senate of the State of Franklin and later its secretary of state. The county seat was named for Landon Carter's wife Elizabeth.

Elizabethton was located on land belonging to Samuel Tipton in whose home the court met until a log courthouse was built. A more substantial building lasted from 1820 until 1852 when the present antebellum courthouse was constructed. Plans were drawn by Joseph S. Burts for a three-story building; the contract went to John Lyle and William M. Flemming for $7,100. Much of this courthouse was rebuilt after a fire in 1932. Extensive renovations were completed in 1986. In 1994, new courtroom facilities were added. Reedy & Sykes were the architects.

The courthouse is in the Elizabethton Historic District which is on the National Register of Historic Places.

Census: 1850—6,296 (Whites 5,911; Free Blacks 32; Slaves 353); 1950—42,432; 1990—51,505 (Whites 50,763; African Americans 456; Native Americans 91; Asians 144; Hispanics 191)

Per capita income (1991): $11,886; 62 percent of national average

Land area: 341 square miles; drained by the Watauga River

National Historic Landmark: Sycamore Shoals, Watauga River

Of interest: Milligan College; Roan Mountain State Resort Park, 1,450 acres. Governor Robert Love Taylor (1850–1912), Democrat, served from 1887–1891 and 1897–1899; Governor Alfred Alexander Taylor (1848–1931), Republican, served from 1921–1923. Governors Robert and Al Taylor were brothers belonging to opposing parties. They ran against each other in a campaign known as the "War of the Roses."

 **Cheatham County** was established in 1856; named for Edward S. Cheatham, speaker of the Tennessee legislature, 1855–1861. Ashland City received its name from the numerous ash trees in the vicinity.

A log building at Sycamore Powder Mills was used in 1856 for the first two sessions of the court. (A cabin has been built across the street from the elementary school in Ashland City using logs from the original courthouse.) The court then met in the Leeland Meeting House at Forest Hill until 1858 when a two-story frame courthouse was erected for $2000 in Ashland City. In 1869 a brick courthouse was built for $12,000. In 1914 the present courthouse was constructed at a cost of $25,000; the 1869 building was utilized as the rear section. R. E. Tubeville was the architect; Slayden and McNabb, the contractors. In 1986 a Criminal Justice Center addition was built, partly surrounding the back of the 1869 courthouse. John Coleman Hayes & Associates Inc. were the architects; Phillips Swager Associates, architects/engineers. The Cheatham County Courthouse is on the National Register of Historic Places.

Census: 1870—6,678; 1970—9,167; 1990—27,140 (Whites 26,460; African Americans 534; Native Americans 84; Asians 36; Hispanics 139)

Per capita income (1991): $14,231; 74 percent of the national average

Land area: 303 square miles; drained by the Harpeth and Cumberland Rivers

National Historic Landmark: Patterson Forge, Montgomery Bell Tunnel, Narrows of the Harpeth. Montgomery Bell, prior to 1820, excavated a 290-foot tunnel (with a fall of 16 feet) through the ridge at the Narrows of the Harpeth River in order to provide water for his iron works.

Of interest: Cheatham Lake.

Chester County was established in

1879; though first designated Wisdom County (by the legislature in 1875), it was named Chester County in honor of Colonel Robert I. Chester, veteran of the War of 1812. The county seat, known as Dayton prior to the Civil War, was named for Colonel James Henderson, veteran of the War of 1812.

Chester County had three court-houses. The first (1883–1891) was formerly the home of Dr. J. A. Crook and burned. The second (1891–1910) also burned. The present court-house, which is on the National Register of Historic Places, was built in 1913; brick veneer was added in 1955. Colonel Chester, for whom the county was named, gave the bell.

A major skirmish took place during the Civil War when Confederate General Joe Wheeler, in a surprise raid, captured the Union defense with all supplies and escaped across the Tennessee River with Federal troops in hot pursuit.

The western part of the county was called "Hurst Nation" because of the numerous members in the area of the staunchly Unionist Hurst family.

Census: 1890—9,053; 1950—11,149; 1990—12,819 (Whites 11,355; African Americans 1,412; Native Americans 20; Asians 22; Hispanics 53)

Per capita income (1991): $11,826; 62 percent of national average

Land area: 289 square miles; drained by the Forked Deer River

Of interest: Chickasaw State Rustic Park, 11,215 acres; Freed-Hardeman University. Eddie Arnold, famous popular singer, was from Chester County.

Claiborne County was established in 1801; named for William C. C. Claiborne, then governor of the Mississippi Territory, judge of the Superior Court of Tennessee, and congressman from Tennessee; he later became governor of Louisiana. The county seat, Tazewell, was named for a well-known Virginia family.

The courts were held in the homes of magistrates until 1804 when the first courthouse was built. The second courthouse, built around 1850, was burned in 1862 by Confederate troops. A third courthouse, built in 1867, was burned in 1932.

The present courthouse was completed in 1933 for $150,000. Bauman & Bauman were the architects; V. L. Nicholson Co., general contractor. A road, following the famous route pioneered by Daniel Boone, was built through the Cumberland Gap in 1796. The last hanging in the county was in 1875 when Ananias Honeycutt publicly met his fate.

Census: 1850—9,369 (Whites 8,610; Free Blacks 99; Slaves 660); **1950**—24,788; **1990**—26,137 (Whites 25,701; African Americans 250; Native Americans 56; Asians 112; Hispanics 83)

Per capita income (1991): $13,046; 68 percent of national average

Land area: 434 square miles; drained by the Powell and Clinch Rivers

Of interest: Cumberland Gap National Historic Park; Lincoln Memorial University. Coal mining is a major industry; much of the county's mineral rights are said to be owned by the British royal family.

Claiborne County Seat—Tazewell, Tennessee 37879

Clay County was established in 1870; named in honor of Henry Clay, congressman and senator from Kentucky, speaker of the House of Representatives, secretary of state under President John Quincy Adams, and three times a candidate for president. Celina was named for a daughter of the pioneer educator, Moses Fisk.

The present courthouse, which is on the National Register of Historic Places, was built in 1872 for $9,999 by D. L. Dow, Cookeville contractor. The courtroom is furnished with the original handmade "pews."

Free Hills was a settlement of blacks who, prior to the Civil War, were given their freedom and four hundred acres of land. They adopted the name of Hill from their former owner.

Great rafts of logs were floated down the Obey and the Cumberland Rivers from Celina to Nashville in the days when the virgin forests were being felled.

Census: 1880—6,987; 1950—8,701; 1990—7,238 (Whites 7,103; African Americans 116; Native Americans 11; Asians 3; Hispanics 27)

Per capita income (1991): $12,604; 66 percent of national average

Land area: 236 square miles; drained by the Obey and Cumberland Rivers

Of interest: Dale Hollow Dam and Lake.

Clay County Seat—Celina, Tennessee 38551

Cocke County was established in 1797; named in honor of William Cocke, officer of the Revolutionary War, leader of the State of Franklin and, with William Blount, one of the first U.S. senators from Tennessee.

The first courthouse was built of logs in 1799 in "Oldtown" on the French Broad River. The second courthouse, built of handmade brick in 1828, was used until 1868 when the county seat was moved to Clifton (now Newport) on the Pigeon River. The third courthouse was a rented one which burned in 1876. The county seat then moved back to Oldtown to the 1828 courthouse. In 1884 the county seat returned to Newport, and a courthouse costing $10,000 was built.

The present courthouse was built in 1930 for $110,000. Manley and Young of Knoxville were the architects; H. C. Fonde & Sons, the contractor. The Cocke County Courthouse is on the National Register of Historic Places.

Census: 1850—8,300 (Whites 7,501; Free Blacks 80; Slaves 719); **1950**—22,991; **1990**—29,141 (Whites 28,398; African Americans 618; Native Americans 78; Asians 31; Hispanics 144)

Per capita income (1991): $11,658; 61 percent of the national average

Land area: 434 square miles; drained by the French Broad and Pigeon Rivers

Of interest: Cherokee National Forest; Foot Hills National Parkway; Great Smoky Mountains National Park, 511,714 acres. Governor Ben W. Hooper (1870–1957), Republican, served from 1911–1915. A crime fighter, he almost lost his life to an assassin.

In 1974 the courthouse was the scene of a famous snake-handling trial. *Christy*, the book and popular 1994 television series, is based on life in the Del Rio community of Cocke County.

Cocke County Seat—Newport, Tennessee 37821

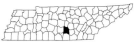 **Coffee County** was established in 1836; named for Major General John Coffee, veteran of the War of 1812, surveyor, close friend of Andrew Jackson. The county seat was named for Manchester, England.

The first courthouse, built of brick in 1837 at the cost of $10,000, burned in 1870. Arson was suspected when a county official was found to be "short" in his books.

The present courthouse was built in 1871–1873 and is on the National Register of Historic Places. Though bid for $12,000, the final cost was $23,071. The builders were J. O. and D. S. Wright and Henry Levy.

The building was funded with taxes on property, "shows, circuses, concerts, and drummers [salesmen]." This courthouse was extensively renovated in 1973 after a lively argument between those dedicated to saving this historic building and those who would like to build a modern facility (estimated cost over $1.8 million).

Census: 1850—8,351 (Whites 7,074; Free Blacks 10; Slaves 1,267); **1950**—23,431; **1990**—40,339 (Whites 38,459; African Americans 1,493; Native Americans 84; Asians 251; Hispanics 261)

Per capita income (1991): $15,755; 82 percent of national average

Land area: 429 square miles; drained by the Duck River

Of interest: Arnold Engineering Development Center; Old Stone Fort State Archaeological Area; Normandy Lake; University of Tennessee Space Institute. George Dickels Distillery in Tullahoma makes Tennessee's "best" whiskey.

Crockett County was established

in 1871; named for David Crockett, famous frontiersman, U.S. congressman, killed at the Alamo in San Antonio, Texas, in 1836. "Remember the Alamo" became an historic war cry.

The present courthouse is the original one built in 1871. The architect was John Archer of Brownsville. Remodeling in 1934 removed the clock tower.

Robert H. White, Ph.D. (1883–1970), author, humorist, lecturer and Tennessee's first official state historian, was a native of Crockett County.

Census: 1880—14,109; 1950—16,624; 1990—13,378 (Whites 11,097; African Americans 2,252; Native Americans 9; Asians 9; Hispanics 49)

Per capita income (1991): $13,529; 71 percent of the national average

Land area: 265 square miles; drained by the Forked Deer River.

Crockett County Seat—Alamo, Tennessee 38001

Cumberland County was established in 1856; named for the Cumberland

Mountains which were named for the Duke of Cumberland by Dr. Thomas Walker, an early explorer. Crossville was at the intersection of the Old Stock Road (north-south from Kentucky to Alabama and Georgia), the Walton Road from the east, and several westbound stage roads.

The first courthouse was a log structure used until 1886 and then sold for $25. The second, built of native sandstone for $5,200, served from 1886 to 1905; when it burned, records stored in the vault survived. J. F. Bowman was the architect; D. G. Brown, the contractor. The third courthouse, built in 1905 of Indiana limestone, cost approximately $23,000. W. Chamberlin & Company was the architect; Lewman & Company of Louisville, the contractor. Renovations in 1978 were by Hart, Freeland & Roberts and the Flynn Construction Company. The Cumberland County

Courthouse is on the National Register of Historic Places.

Census: 1870—3,461; **1950**—18,877; **1990**—34,736 (Whites 34,475; African Americans 42; Native Americans 137; Asians 49; Hispanics 124)

Per capita income (1991): $12,880; 67 percent of the national average

Land area: 682 square miles; drained by the Cumberland and Tennessee Rivers

Of interest: Cumberland Mountain State Rustic Park, 1,720 acres; Cumberland Plateau; Cumberland Playhouse, Crossville; Homestead Tower.

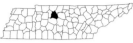

Davidson County was established in 1783; named in honor of Brigadier General William Lee Davidson of North Carolina, distinguished Revolutionary officer killed in 1781 at the battle of Cowan's Ford, North Carolina. Nashville was named for General Francis Nash who was killed during the Revolution at the battle of Germantown, Pennsylvania.

Nashville was designated the permanent state capital of Tennessee in October 1843. Prior to this, the capital had been in Knoxville 1796–1811, Nashville 1812–1815, Knoxville 1817–1818, Murfreesboro 1819–1825, and back in Nashville since 1827. The state legislature met in Kingston for one day, September 21, 1807 (see Roane County).

There have been five Davidson County Courthouses. The first, authorized by the 1783 court, was 18 feet square of hewn logs and burned in 1796. Prior to the building of the second courthouse, a Methodist church was used. The second courthouse was built of bricks in 1802. The third courthouse, a three-story structure with cupola and bell built in 1830 for approximately $14,000, burned in 1856. The fourth, "Strickland Courthouse," was designed by W. F. (Francis) Strickland, son of the famous William Strickland, architect for the state capitol. Built in 1857 for $90,000, an additional story was added in 1910.

The present courthouse, funded in part by the Federal Emergency Administration of Public Works, was built in 1937 at a cost of approximately $1,595,000 and is listed on the National Register of Historical Places. Emmons H. Woolwine of

Nashville and Frederick C. Hirons of New York were the architects. John Howard Clark moved to Nashville from New York to supervise the construction. The mural paintings were done by Dean Cornwell; the decorative paintings, by George Davidson.

In 1962 Davidson County merged with Nashville to become the Metropolitan Government of Nashville and Davidson County. The Davidson County/Metropolitan Courthouse is on the National Register of Historic Places.

Census: 1850—38,882 (Whites 23,853; Free Blacks 854; Slaves 14,175); **1950**—321,758; **1990**—510,784 (Whites 381,740; African Americans 119,273; Native Americans 1,162; Asians 7,081; Hispanics 4,775)

Per capita income (1991): $20,296; 106 percent of the national average

Land area: 502 square miles; drained by the Cumberland River

Historic National Landmarks: Downtown Presbyterian Church; George Peabody College for Teachers (Vanderbilt University); The Hermitage; Jubilee Hall (Fisk University); Nashville Union Station and Trainshed; Tennessee State Capitol

Colleges: American Baptist Theological Seminary; Aquinas College; Belmont College; David Lipscomb University; Fisk University; Free Will Baptist College; Meharry Medical College; Tennessee State University; Trevecca Nazarene College; Vanderbilt University

Of interest: Belle Meade Plantation; Centennial Park (The Parthenon); Country Music Hall of Fame; Cumberland Science Museum; Grand Ole Opry; J. Percy Priest Lake; Fort Nashborough; Fort Negley; Music Row; Nashville Symphony Orchestra; Old Hickory Lake and Locks; Opryland; Opryland Hotel; Radnor Lake; Ryman Auditorium; Tennessee Botanical Gardens & Fine Arts Center at Cheekwood; Tennessee State Museum; Warner Park, Travellers' Rest. Governor William Carroll (1788–1844), Democrat, served 1821–1827 and 1829–1835; Governor Aaron V. Brown (1795–1859), Democrat, served 1845–1847; Governor Hill McAlister (1875–1960), Democrat, served 1933–1937.

 *Decatur County* was established in 1845; named for Commodore Stephen Decatur, hero of the war with Tripoli, who won fame when he recaptured the frigate *Philadelphia*. He also served in the War of 1812. He is remembered for the toast, "Our country! In her intercourse with foreign nations may she always be in the right, but our country, right or wrong."

The first log courthouse was built in Decaturville in 1848. It was replaced shortly by a frame building which burned in 1869. A two-story brick courthouse, built in 1869 for $9000, burned in 1927. The present courthouse was built in 1928 by Elston Tate, architect and contractor. A $200,000 "face-lifting" was carried out in 1975.

Paleontologists have found fossils in Decatur County of fish, shell-forming sea animals, reef-building corals, and sponges of the Silurian period of the Paleozoic era.

Census: 1850—6,003 (Whites 5,263; Free Blacks 17; Slaves 723); **1950**—9,442; **1990**—10,472 (Whites 10,000; African Americans 417; Native Americans 23; Asians 21; Hispanics 49)

Per capita income (1991): $11,999; 63 percent of the national average

Land area: 333 square miles; bounded on the east by Kentucky Lake/Tennessee River

Of interest: Brownsport Furnace I & II; Decatur Furnace; Mouse Tail Landing State Rustic Park.

Decatur County Seat—Decaturville, Tennessee 38329

 **DeKalb County** was established in 1837; named in honor of Baron Johann DeKalb, a Bavarian officer who accompanied LaFayette to America in 1777 and was killed in the Battle of Camden in 1780. The county seat was named for the Honorable Samuel Granville Smith, Tennessee secretary of state 1831–1835.

There have been four courthouses. The first was built in 1840. Others were built in 1890, 1925, and 1971. The 1890 courthouse burned in 1925; the records were preserved. It had no fence, and people complained that "hogs often slept in the hall and that Mrs. Scott Tyree's geese roosted on the steps." The 1971 courthouse cost $750,000. The architect was Maffett-Howland and Associates; builder, M. T. Puckett Construction Co.

Census: 1850—8,016 (Whites 7,331; Free Blacks 17; Slaves 668); **1950**—11,680; **1990**—14,360 (Whites 14,074; African Americans 215; Native Americans 19; Asians 12; Hispanics 62)

Per capita income (1991): $13,471; 70 percent of the national average

Land area: 304 square miles, drained by the Caney Fork River

Of interest: Center Hill Lake; Edgar Evins State Rustic Park, 6000 acres.

 *Dickson County* was established in 1803; named in honor of Dr. William Dickson, a Nashville physician, speaker of the Tennessee House of Representatives, and a U.S. congressman from 1801–1807. The county seat was named for Charlotte Robertson, wife of James Robertson, the "Father of Tennessee."

The present courthouse has the distinction of being the oldest courthouse in use in the state and is on the National Register of Historic Places. It was built by Phillip Murry in 1831–1833 after the first courthouse of 1812 was destroyed by the tornado that demolished the town of Charlotte in 1830. In 1930 wings were added and, because it was not possible to match the original brick, the whole building was encased in brick that matched the new wings. To quote, "Today, hidden by a shield of bricks, the oldest courthouse in Tennessee stands on a hillside in the quiet little town of Charlotte" (Herbert L. Harper, "The Antebellum Courthouses of Tennessee," *Tennessee Historical Quarterly*, Spring 1971). In 1977 the courthouse complex was greatly enlarged by the construction across the square of a Dickson County building. In 1899 by act of the legislature, the county business was divided between Charlotte and the industrial town of Dickson; circuit and chancery courts were held in Dickson; county court in Charlotte. A courthouse was built in Dickson. In 1927 by referendum, Charlotte was designated the sole county seat.

Census: 1850—8,404 (Whites 6,285; Free Blacks 1; Slaves 2,118); **1950**—18,805; **1990**—35,061 (Whites 33,145; African Americans 1,744; Native Americans 68; Asians 71; Hispanics 177)

Per capita income (1991): $15,489; 81 percent of the national average

Land area: 490 square miles; drained by Harpeth and Cumberland Rivers

Of interest: Cheatham Lake/ Cumberland River; Montgomery Bell State Resort Park. Governor Frank G. Clement (1920–1969), Democrat, served 1953–1959 and 1963–1967.

 **Dyer County** was established in 1823; named for Colonel Robert Henry Dyer, veteran of the War of 1812, the Seminole War, the Natchez Expedition, and the Creek War. The county seat also bears Colonel Dyer's name.

There have been six courthouses in Dyersburg. The first, a double-log building with dirt floor, was used from 1824 to 1827. The second (1828–1836) was a two-story log structure erected on the public square. The third (1836–1850) was a one-story frame building. The fourth two-story brick courthouse (1850–1864) was burned by a Confederate soldier and rebuilt in 1867 for approximately $8000. The present sixth courthouse was built in 1911 by Asa Briggs. Major renovations took place in 1969 and in 1988. The Dyer County Courthouse is on the National Register of Historic Places.

> **Census: 1850**—6,361 (Whites 4,884; Free Blacks 9; Slaves 1,468); **1950**—33,473; **1990**—34,854 (Whites 30,541; African Americans 4,145; Native Americans 64; Asians 63; Hispanics 137)
>
> **Per capita income (1991):** $15,024; 78 percent of the national average
>
> **Land area:** 510 square miles; drained by the Mississippi River
>
> **Of interest:** Moss Island Waterfowl Refuge; Tigrett Wildlife Management Area.

Fayette County was established in 1824; named for Marquis de LaFayette, French nobleman and distinguished soldier who rendered invaluable service to the American cause during the Revolutionary War. The county seat was named for Lieutenant Robert Somerville who fought under General Andrew Jackson and was killed in 1814 at the Battle of Horseshoe Bend.

Fayette County has had four courthouses: a log courthouse in 1825; a brick structure in 1833; and a building in 1876 that cost $45,000 and burned in 1925. The present courthouse (George Mahan Jr., architect) was built in 1925 and is on the National Register of Historic Places. Extensive renovation in 1983–1985 cost $250,000, Grace & Associates, architects; Vanderhayden Construction Company, contractor. In 1984 a fourteen-foot spire of grey Georgian granite was erected to honor all Fayette County veterans.

Census: 1850—26,719 (Whites 11,416; Free Blacks 39; Slaves 15,264); **1950**—27,535; **1990**—25,559 (Whites 14,204; African Americans 11,295; Native Americans 33; Asians 15; Hispanics 130)

Per capita income (1991): $13,054; 68 percent of the national average

Land area: 705 square miles. Drained by the Wolf, Hatchie, and Loosahatchie Rivers

Of interest: Ames Plantation; Herb Parsons Lake.

Fentress County was established in 1823; named for James Fentress, speaker, for four terms, of the Tennessee House of Representatives. Jamestown (nicknamed "Jim Town") became the county seat in 1828 and derived its name from the first name of James Fentress for whom the county is named.

The first courthouse was built in 1828 and burned in 1860. The second courthouse burned in 1904. The present courthouse, built in 1906, was greatly enlarged and renovated in 1974. Clemmons & Gingles were the engineers; Blair & Blair, the contractors.

The Jamestown area was noted for its many springs; the community was originally named Sandy Springs.

John Clemens, father of Samuel L. Clemens (Mark Twain) and a large landowner, was one of the commissioners who helped develop plans for the county's first courthouse.

Sergeant York, 1887–1964, was a famous World War I hero who was awarded the Medal of Honor.

Census: 1850—4,454 (Whites 4,305; Free Blacks 1; Slaves 148); **1950**—14,917; **1990**—14,669 (Whites 14,636; African Americans 2; Native Americans 10; Asians 18; Hispanics 39)

Per capita income (1991): $10,468; 55 percent of the national average

Land area: 499 square miles; drained by the Obey, Clear Fork, Wolf, and Clear Creek Rivers

National Historic Landmark: Sergeant Alvin Cullom York Farm and Grist Mill at Pall Mall

Of interest: Big South Fork National River Recreational Area (also in Scott County); Dale Hollow Lake; Forbus General Store annual fireworks display, July 4th; Pickett State Rustic Park.

Franklin County was established

in 1807; named in honor of Benjamin Franklin, one of the founding fathers of America. The county seat was named for General James Winchester, one of the founders of Memphis.

The first courthouse, 1807–1814, was a one-room log cabin in Cowan. A small brick courthouse was built in Winchester in 1818 on land purchased for one dollar from a man named Christopher Bullard. Funds for the building were raised by lottery. In 1839 this courthouse was replaced at a cost of $10,000; Elish Merideth, the builder. Fighting took place around the courthouse during the Civil War. A new courthouse, built in 1890, was replaced in 1937; Marr and Holman of Nashville, were the architects; Nile Yearwood of Nashville, the contractor. The Franklin County Courthouse is on the National Register of Historic Places.

Census: 1850—13,768 (Whites 10,085; Free Blacks 60; Slaves 3,623); **1950**—25,341; **1990**—34,725 (Whites 32,425; African Americans 2,095; Native Americans 55; Asians 95; Hispanics 187)

Per capita income (1991): $12,143; 63 percent of the national average

Land area: 553 square miles, drained by the Elk River

Of interest: Carter Caves State Natural Area; Cumberland Mountain Tunnel; Dick Cove National Natural Landmark; Franklin-Marion State Forest; Natural Bridge at Sewanee; Tim's Ford State Rustic Park; University of the South at Sewanee. Governor Isham G. Harris (1818–1897), Democrat, served 1857–1862; Governor Albert S. Marks (1836–1897), Democrat, served 1879–1881.

 **Gibson County** was established in 1823; named for Colonel John Gibson who served in the Creek Wars and the War of 1812. Trenton was named for Trenton, New Jersey, near the home of Colonel Gibson. In 1868 Gibson County was divided by a private act of the legislature into two jurisdictions and is one of two counties that has courthouses in two cities (see Washington County).

Trenton has had four courthouses. The first was a hewed-log building, 20 by 35 feet, built in 1825 and replaced in 1829 by a two-story brick structure that cost approximately $6000. The third courthouse was completed in 1841 for $20,000. The present courthouse was built in 1899–1901 for $85,000. W. Chamberlin & Company of Knoxville were the architects; T. R. Biggs & Son, the builder. Though the clock tower was destroyed by fire in 1941, it was promptly rebuilt; a bell rings the hour. The Gibson County Courthouse is on the National Register of Historic Places. A bust of David Crockett, a Confederate monument, and a fountain in memory of Leo Freed are prominent on the grounds.

Cases occurring south of a line passing through the community of Fruitland are tried in Humboldt; cases north of the line are tried in the county seat of Trenton. The court in Humboldt, which originally met in the old city hall, now meets in the newly renovated Municipal Center. Some out-of-county lawyers have had their cases dismissed when they failed to appear at the right district court (Trenton rather than Humboldt or vice versa).

Census: 1850—19,548 (Whites 15,286; Free blacks 68; Slaves 4,194); **1950**—48,132; **1990**—46,315 (Whites 37,237; African Americans 8,944; Native Americans 37; Asians 61; Hispanics 181)

Per capita income (1991): $14,575; 76 percent of the national average

Land area: 603 square miles; drained by the Obion and Forked Deer Rivers

Of interest: The Crockett Cabin in Rutherford was Davy Crockett's last home in Tennessee.

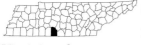 *Giles County* was established in 1809; named for Senator William B. Giles of Virginia, who was a strong advocate for the admission of Tennessee to the Union. The county seat was named for Count Kazimierz Pulaski (1747–1779), the Polish hero who joined the American Revolution and died as a result of wounds received in Savannah, Georgia.

Giles County has had six courthouses. The first two courthouses were built of logs: in 1810, in Lewis Kirk's settlement on Richland Creek; in 1811, after the public square was cleared of dense cane. The second courthouse burned after two years. The third courthouse, a two-story brick structure built by Archibald Alexander, was used until the 1850s. The fourth courthouse, built in 1856, was said to be the "finest in the state"; however, due to a faulty flue, it burned soon after completion. The fifth courthouse, a two-story brick building with cupola and bell was designed by Adolphus Heiman. The courthouse was built in 1857 at a cost of $27,000 and was destroyed by fire in 1907. Federal troops occupied this building during the Civil War. The present courthouse, which is on the National Register of Historic Places, was completed in 1909 and cost $137,000 with furnishings. Benjamin B. Smith of Montgomery, Alabama,

was the architect; George Moore & Sons of Nashville were the builders.

Prominent on the courthouse square is the monument to Sam Davis, a young Confederate spy ("Coleman Scout"). He was hanged two blocks east of the courthouse in 1863 by Federal troops when he refused to reveal the source of the information he carried in his boots.

Census: 1850—25,949 (Whites 16,518; Free Blacks 73; Slaves 9,358); **1950**—26,961; **1990**—25,741 (Whites 22,184; African Americans 3,405; Native Americans 57; Asians 61; Hispanics 109)

Per capita income (1991): $14,092; 74 percent of the national average

Land area: 611 square miles; drained by the Elk River and Richland Creek

Of interest: Governor Neill S. Brown (1810-86), Whig, served 1847–1849; Governor John Calvin Brown (1827–1889), Whig/Democrat, who served 1871–1875; these governors were brothers.

Grainger County was established

in 1796; named for Mary Grainger, wife of William Blount. The county seat was named for George Rutledge, a prominent pioneer.

The court was held in various places between 1796–1801. Grainger County has had four courthouses. The first courthouse was built in 1801 and later purchased by the Presbyterian Church. The second courthouse, a small brick structure, was built in 1848. The third courthouse, built in 1904 for $24,000 (architect, Wheeler & Runge; builder, M. J. Lewman & Co.) burned in 1946. The present courthouse was built in 1949 at a cost of $300,000. Bauman & Bauman, were the architects; Johnson & Wilder, the contractors.

Census: 1850—12,370 (Whites 11,170; Free Blacks 165; Slaves 1,035); **1950**—13,086; **1990**—17,095 (Whites 16,939; African Americans 102; Native Americans 42; Asians 8; Hispanics 41)

Per capita income (1991): $10,700; 56 percent of the national average

Land area: 280 square miles; drained by the Clinch and Holston Rivers

Of interest: Cherokee Lake; Trail of the Lonesome Pine State Scenic Trail. President Andrew Johnson's first tailor shop sits on the courthouse grounds.

Grainger County Seat—Rutledge, Tennessee 37861

Greene County was established in 1783; named for Nathaniel Greene, major general in the Revolutionary Army. Greene County was the last capital of the State of Franklin. Greeneville was the home of Andrew Johnson (1808–1875), who became president of the United States from 1865 to 1869 upon the assassination of Abraham Lincoln.

Greene County has had three courthouses. The first, built in 1783 of logs, was used until 1836 when a colonial brick courthouse was built by Thomas Crutchfield. The present courthouse was built in 1916 for $40,000. Thomas S. Brown, was the architect; N. H. Franklin, the contractor. The courthouse grounds contain both a Confederate monument and a statue honoring a Federal soldier; the only county to pay tribute to both sides in this way.

Census: 1850—17,824 (Whites 16,526; Free Blacks 205; Slaves 1,093); **1950**—41,048; **1990**—55,853 (Whites 54,440; African Americans 1,223; Native Americans 89; Asians 70; Hispanics 163)

Per capita income (1991): $13,318; 69 percent of the national average

Land area: 622 square miles; drained by Lick Creek and the Nolichucky River

Of interest: Andrew Johnson Historic Site; David Crockett's Birthplace Park; Tusculum College. Andrew Johnson served as governor of Tennessee (1853–1857), Civil War military governor (1862–1865), U.S. congressman, and U.S. senator before becoming the seventeenth U.S. president.

 **Grundy County** was established in 1844 and named in honor of Felix Grundy, U.S. senator and congressman, and attorney general in the cabinet of President Van Buren. Altamont became the county seat in 1848. Known as Wooten Cabins, it was a place where stockmen met and salted their cattle on the "wide range." Prior to 1848, court was held at Beersheba Springs.

The first courthouse burned in 1882. The courthouse built in 1885 was destroyed by arson May 3, 1990. A new courthouse on Cumberland Street, approximately one block southwest of the original structure, was completed in 1995 at a cost of $1,322,300. The architect was Richard C. Williams; contractor, Peery Construction Company.

While Altamont remained the official seat of justice, a branch circuit court was located in Tracy City from 1913–1957.

Census: 1850—2,773 (Whites 2,522; Free Blacks 15; Slaves 236); **1950**—12,558; **1990**—13,362 (Whites 13,294; African Americans 19; Native Americans 28; Asians 6; Hispanics 68)

Per capita income (1991): $11,034; 58 percent of the national average

Land area: 361 square miles; drained by numerous small streams

Of interest: Beersheba Springs Historic District; South Cumberland Recreational Area which includes the Stone Door/Savage Gulf complex.

Hamblen County was established in 1870; named for Hezekiah Hamblen of Hawkins County. Morristown was named for the Morris family, early settlers of the area.

The courthouse is the original one built in 1874 at a cost of $21,750 and is on the National Register of Historic Places. A. C. Bruce was the architect; George Folsom and John Lyle, were the builders. Renovation was carried out in 1956 and again in 1968–1969. The 1969 renovation cost $300,000. Price Denton Associate, of Community Tectonics, Inc., was the architect; Carton Construction Company of Morristown, the builders. In 1993 renovations, costing $125,000 were carried out by Price & Price Mechanical Air Conditioning.

The courthouse originally had two windowless "dungeon cells" on the ground floor. A certain Anthony Blair, who was convicted of murdering some of his family, was confined in the dungeon until he was hanged September 26, 1879. Two doctors were reported to have paid $15 for his body for medical study. According to a local newspaper, this is the only hanging recorded in Hamblen County.

> **Census: 1880**—10,187; **1950**—23,967; **1990**—50,480 (Whites 47,891; African Americans 2,323; Native Americans 85; Asians 128; Hispanics 175)
>
> **Per capita income (1991):** $14,629; 77 percent of the national average
>
> **Land area:** 161 square miles; drained by the Holston and French Broad Rivers
>
> **Of interest:** Cherokee Lake; David Crockett Tavern and Museum (Morristown); Panther Creek State Recreational Park (1,400 acres).

HAMILTON COUNTY COURTHOUSE

Hamilton County was established

in 1819; named for Alexander Hamilton, secretary of the treasury under President George Washington. The city of Chattanooga developed into an industrial and transportation center after the Civil War. The Indian word *chattanooga* means "rock coming to a point." First known as Ross's Landing, Chattanooga was not incorporated until 1858. The county seat, first located in Dallas, moved to Harrison in 1840 where a substantial brick courthouse was built by Thomas Crutchfield Sr. In 1870 the county seat moved to Chattanooga. Controversy over this move resulted in the formation of James County which existed from 1870 until 1920.

In Chattanooga, the county court used existing buildings until 1879 when an imposing structure was built of brick for $100,325 by A. C. Bruce, architect, and Patton & McInturf, contractor. This courthouse was destroyed by fire in 1910 when struck by lightening. The present fireproof building (of Tennessee marble with glazed tile roof and colored glass dome) was completed in 1913 for $350,000. R. H. Hunt of Chattanooga was the architect; George A. Fuller, the contractor. The courthouse is on the National Register of Historic Places.

The newest addition to the courthouse complex (1975–1976) is a six-story Criminal Justice Building costing $7,486,582.44. Jack H. Tyler was the architect. The lobby contains an oval-shaped bronze "transcendental symbolic sculpture" titled *Good and Evil*, hand-forged by the famous Mexican sculptor, Victor Manuel Conteras. On the grounds, statues honor Confederate General A. P. Stewart, and John Ross (1790–1866), "Indian Chief, Loyal Cherokee, Great American."

Census: 1850—10,075 (Whites 9,216; Free Blacks 187; Slaves 672); **1950**—208,255; **1990**—285,536 (Whites 227,413; African Americans 54,477; Native Americans 585; Asians 2,479; Hispanics 1,946)

Per capita income (1991): $18,788; 98 percent of the national average

Land area: 543 square miles; drained by the Tennessee River

National Historic Landmark: Moccasin Bend Archaeological District

Colleges: Southern College; Tennessee Temple University; University of Tennessee at Chattanooga

Of interest: Booker T. Washington State Park; Chattanooga "Choo-Choo" Railway Museum; Chattanooga Regional History Museum; Chickamauga and Chattanooga National Military Park; Chickamauga Lake; Craven's House on Lookout Mountain; Harrison Bay State Park; Hunter Museum of Art; The Houston Museum; Lookout Mountain Incline Railway; Lookout Point Park; Nickajack Lake; Rock City Gardens; Ruby Falls; Sequoyah Nuclear Plant; Tennessee Aquarium; Walnut Street Bridge.

Hancock County was established in 1844; named for John Hancock, a member of the Continental Congress and first signer of the Declaration of Independence. Sneedville, first called Greasy Rock, was named for L. T. Sneed, the eminent lawyer who successfully defended the new county in the suit brought against it for running the county line within twelve miles of Rogersville, the county seat of Hawkins County.

The first court was held in the home of Alexander Campbell in Union Church until the courthouse was built in Sneedville. The small substantial brick courthouse burned in 1850 with all its contents. The present courthouse was built in 1931. Allen N. Dryden was the architect; Emory Construction Company, the builders. Each post of the fence surrounding the courthouse is named for a local citizen. One of the first counties in the state to establish a public school system; telephones were installed in 1939; electricity, in 1941.

Census: 1850—5,660 (Whites 5,447; Free Blacks 11; Slaves 202); **1950**—9,116; **1990**—6,739 (Whites 6,596; African Americans 122; Native Americans 18; Asians 1; Hispanics 35)

Per capita income (1991): $9,761; 51 percent of the national average

Land area: 222 square miles; drained by the Clinch River

Of interest: "Walk Toward the Sunset," an outdoor drama produced each summer; Old Jail, National Register of Historic Places. The Melungeons, a swarthy people of unknown origin, live in the deep valleys of the county.

Hancock County Seat—Sneedville, Tennessee 37869

Hardeman County was established in 1823; named for Colonel Thomas Jones Hardeman, who served with Andrew Jackson at the Battle of New Orleans in the War of 1812. The county seat, first known as *Hatchie Town*, was named for Simon Bolivar, the liberator of Venezuela.

The first courthouse, a two-story log structure, was built in 1824 on the square. In 1827 it was bought by Levi Joy and is known today as the "Joy-Hardaway House." The second courthouse, built of bricks in 1827, was burned by Federal troops in 1864. The present courthouse was built in 1868; Willis, Sloan, & Trigg, architects. Additions were made in 1955; Eason, Anthony, McNinnie & Cox, architects; Forcum-James Company, builders. Renovation in 1978 cost $450,000; Hart, Freeland & Roberts were the architect/engineers; Morris Construction Company, the contractor. A bust of Simon Bolivar, presented by the government of Venezuela, stands in front of the courthouse. The Bolivar Court Square Historic District is listed on the National Register of Historic Places.

Census: 1850—17,456 (Whites 10,308; Free Blacks 40; Slaves 7,108); **1950**—23,313; **1990**—23,377 (Whites 14,536; African Americans 8,748; Native Americans 20; Asians 62; Hispanics 175)

Per capita income (1991): $12,573; 66 percent of the national average

Land area: 668 square miles; drained by the Big Hatchie River

National Historic Landmark: Siege and Battle of Corinth

Of interest: Chickasaw State Park and Forest, 11,215 acres.

 *Hardin County* was established in 1819; named for Colonel Joseph Hardin, Revolutionary War veteran who received a land grant of 2000 acres located in what became Hardin County. Hardin was speaker of the State of Franklin Assembly and speaker of the House of Representatives in the Second Territorial Assembly. It is believed that Colonel Hardin may have surveyed the land as early as 1786. His son James led the first settlers to Hardin County in 1816.

The first court was held at Hardinsville (near Cerro Gordo) in 1820 in the log cabin home of Colonel James Hardin. In 1822 the county seat was moved to Oldtown, then in 1826 to Rudd's Ferry. The county seat in each place was called Hardinsville. In 1827 Rudd's Ferry/Hardinsville was renamed Savannah.

Savannah has had five courthouses. The first of "round gum logs" was used for two years, 1830–1832. A brick courthouse, built in 1832, was burned in the Civil War; the records, however, were saved by the Honorable J. D. Martin. The third courthouse was built in 1867 for $10,000. The fourth courthouse, built in 1906, burned in 1949. The present building, costing $800,000, was completed in 1952. Marr & Holman of Nashville were the architects; Daniels Construction Co. of Birmingham, the builders. The handmade brick was from Glasgow, Virginia; the limestone for steps and pillars, from Bedford, Indiana; marble for the inside stairs and floor, from Italy; entrance-wall finish of volcanic origin, from Vesuvius, Italy; slate shingles, from Vermont. The Savannah Historic District is listed on the National Register of Historic Places.

Census: 1850—10,328 (Whites 9,040; Free Blacks 31; Slaves 1,257); **1950**—16,908; **1990**—22,633 (Whites 21,539; African Americans 997; Native Americans 34; Asians 37; Hispanics 87)

Per capita income (1991): $12,199; 64 percent of the national average

Land area: 578 square miles; drained by the Tennessee River

National Landmark: Shiloh Indian Mounds Site

Of interest: Kentucky Lake; Pickwick Landing State Resort Park (500 acres); Shiloh National Military Park & Cemetery; Tennessee River Museum; Tennessee Waterways Museum. Governor Ray Blanton, Democrat, served from 1975–1979.

Hardin County Seat—Savannah, Tennessee 38372

Hawkins County was established in 1786; named for Benjamin Hawkins, member of the Continental Congress from North Carolina and U.S. senator who signed the Deed of Cession conveying Southwest Territory (now the state of Tennessee) to the federal government. Rogersville was named for Joseph Rogers, an early settler and proprietor of a well-known tavern.

The courthouse, built in 1836–1837, is one of seven Tennessee courthouses still in use that predate the Civil War. The builder was John Dameron of Sullivan County. Renovations in 1929, which included the replacement of the "Dameron cupola" by a "New England steeple," were carried out by Allen N. Dryden of Kingsport for $52,000. This courthouse has gained renown in architectural circles for its brick columns, cornices, Palladian windows, and second-story balcony door. Major renovations were carried out in 1963 by Beeson & Beeson of Johnson City, and in the 1970s a large addition was built onto the rear of the courthouse. The Rogersville Historic District is on the National Register of Historic Places.

Census: **1850**—13,370 (Whites 11,567; Free Blacks 113; Slaves 1,690); **1950**—30,494; **1990**—44,565 (Whites 43,664; African Americans 741; Native Americans 78; Asians 59; Hispanics 134)

Per capita income (1991): $12,434; 65 percent of the national average

Land area: 487 square miles. Drained by the Clinch and Holston Rivers.

Of interest: Cherokee Lake; Hale Springs Inn; Holston U.S. Ordinance Works; John Sevier Lake; Laurel Run Park; Lonesome Pine State Scenic Trail.

Haywood County was established in 1823; named in honor of Judge John Haywood who was judge of the Supreme Court of Errors and Appeals 1816–1826. He was known as the "Father of Tennessee History." Brownsville was named for General Jacob Brown, Revolutionary hero wounded in the battle of Lundy's Lane near Niagara Falls.

The first courthouse, built of logs in 1824, was replaced in 1844 by a brick structure. The bricks were handmade by slave labor. This courthouse was extensively remodeled in 1928 and is one of the seven pre-Civil War courthouses still in use in Tennessee. Courthouse records go back to the 1820s.

The Tennessee Supreme Court (Western Division) held court at the Haywood County Courthouse for one year (1868–1869).

Census: 1850—17,259 (Whites 8,711; Free Blacks 50; Slaves 8,498); **1950**—26,212; **1980**—20,318; **1990**—19,437 (Whites 9,676; African Americans 9,651; Native Americans 24; Asians 19; Hispanics 156)

Per capita income (1991): $13,638; 71 percent of the national average

Land area: 533 square miles; drained by the Hatchie and Forked Deer Rivers

Of interest: The Hatchie State Scenic River in the Hatchie National Wildlife Refuge.

Haywood County Seat—Brownsville, Tennessee 38012

Henderson County was established in 1821; named for Colonel James Henderson, commander of the Tennessee troops in New Orleans in the War of 1812. He was also with General Andrew Jackson on the Natchez Expedition. Lexington was named for Lexington, Massachusetts.

Henderson County has had five courthouses. The first, built of logs in 1822, cost $142. The second, built of brick in 1827 by Samuel Wilson for $587.97, was burned in May 1863 while occupied by Federal troops. The third, built in 1867 by Robert Dyer for $7,450, burned in 1895 with all records. Rebuilt, the fourth courthouse was used until the present courthouse was built in 1961 at a cost of $500,000. Hart, Freeland & Roberts were the architects. In 1994 courthouse renovations totaled $120,000. The architect was Roy L. Scobey of Professional Design Resources.

Census: 1850—13,164 (Whites 10,570; Free Blacks 2; Slaves 2,592); **1950**—17,173; **1990**—21,844 (Whites 19,982; African Americans 1,816; Native Americans 20; Asians 19; Hispanics 100)

Per capita income (1991): $12,858; 67 percent of the national average

Land area: 520 square miles; drained by tributaries of the Tennessee River

Of interest: Natchez Trace State Resort Park & Forest (48,000 acres).

Annual reenactment of the Civil War Battle of Parker's Crossroads (December 31, 1862).

Henderson County Seat—Lexington, Tennessee 38351   51

Henry County was established in 1821; named in honor of Patrick Henry, Revolutionary patriot and statesman who proclaimed, "Give me liberty or give me death."

Henry County has had four courthouses. The first was a two-room log structure built in 1823 by Samuel McCorkle. The second, a two-story brick courthouse built by Burke and McConnell in 1825, was replaced in 1852 by a brick building constructed by Calvin Sweeney for $42,000. The present courthouse was completed in 1897. R. H. Hunt was the architect; E. M.Wallen, the builder. The cupola is covered with bronze. Renovated in 1984, Henry County Courthouse is on the National Register of Historic Places.

Census: 1850—18,233 (Whites 13,387; Free Blacks 25; Slaves 4,821); **1950**—23,828; **1990**—27,888 (Whites 24,955; African Americans 2,813; Native Americans 50; Asians 54; Hispanics 110)

Per capita income (1991): $13,726; 72 percent of the national average

Land area: 562 square miles; bounded on the east by the Kentucky Lake

Of interest: Big Sandy National Wildlife Refuge; Kentucky Lake; Ned R. McWherter Bridge; Paris Landing State Resort Park, 1,200 acres. Governor James Davis Porter (1828–1912), Democrat, served 1875–1879.

Henry County Seat—Paris, Tennessee 38242

Hickman County was established

in 1807; named in honor of Edwin Hickman, "long hunter" and explorer who was killed by Indians in 1791 near the mouth of Defeated Creek on the Duck River not far from Centerville.

The first log courthouse, built in 1808 at Vernon and moved bodily to Centerville in 1823, was destroyed by fire in 1864 to prevent Union troops from taking it. The courthouse was rebuilt after the war, probably in 1868, and was replaced by the present courthouse in 1925–1926. Tisdale, Pinson, & Stone of Nashville were the architects.

Grinder's Switch, two miles from Centerville, was made famous by the late "Minnie Pearl" (Sarah Ophelia Colley Cannon) of country music fame and a native of Hickman County.

Census: 1850—9,397 (Whites 7,559; Free Blacks 22; Slaves 1,816); **1950**—13,353; **1990**—16,754 (Whites 15,831; African Americans 859; Native Americans 40; Asians 8; Hispanics 67)

Per capita income (1991): $12,705; 66 percent of the national average

Land area: 613 square miles; drained by the Duck and Piney Rivers

Of interest: Natchez Trace Parkway (also crosses parts of Wayne, Lawrence, Lewis, Maury, Williamson, and Davidson Counties).

Houston County was established in 1871; named in honor of Sam Houston, congressman from Tennessee 1823–1827 and governor of Tennessee 1827–1829. He moved to Texas, was the first president of the Republic of Texas, and governor of the state of Texas. Erin received its name from the Irish railroad workers who settled in the area.

The first court was held at Union Church in Erin in April 1871 at which time Arlington was selected to be the county seat. The first courthouse, a two-story frame building, was completed in 1872 for $1,440. After much controversy, the county seat was moved to Erin in 1878. A deciding factor was the refusal of the railroad to build a station at Arlington because of the steep grade. The Arlington courthouse became the Arlington Cumberland Presbyterian Church. The courthouse in Erin, a large brick building with a cupola, was completed in 1883 for $8000 by L. J. Neville, builder/architect. The present courthouse, built in 1956–1957 on a new site, cost $185,000. Burkhalter, Hickerson & Associates were the architects; Barrett Construction Company, builders.

Census: 1880—4,295; 1950—5,318; 1990—7,018 (Whites 6,725; African Americans 268; Native Americans 12; Asians 5; Hispanics 41)

Per capita income (1991): $12,691; 66 percent of the national average

Land area: 200 square miles, drained by the Cumberland and Tennessee Rivers

Of interest: Kentucky Lake.

Houston County Seat—Erin, Tennessee 37061

Humphreys County was established in 1809; named for Judge Parry W. Humphreys of the Superior Court of Law and Equity, circuit judge, and congressman. The first county seat was established in 1816 at Reynoldsburg which was named for Congressman John B. Reynolds. When Benton County was established in 1835 from part of Humphreys County, the county seat was moved to Waverly and named for Sir Walter Scott's Waverly novels.

The courthouse at Reynoldsburg, built in 1812–1813, became a private residence in 1837 until it burned in 1940. In Waverly, the first courthouse was built of brick in 1837 for $6000. The second courthouse, built in 1857, burned in 1876. A two-story brick courthouse, built in 1878 by J. P. Pauley of St. Louis for $15,000, burned and was rebuilt in 1898.

The present fifth courthouse was built in 1952 at a cost of $190,000. Steinburg & Wheeler were the architects; Boone Construction Company, the builders.

Census: 1850—6,422 (Whites 5,304; Free Blacks 21; Slaves 1,097); **1950**—11,030; **1990**—15,795 (Whites 15,175; African Americans 551; Native Americans 26; Asians 32; Hispanics 63)

Per capita income (1991): $13,405; 70 percent of the national average

Land area: 532 square miles; drained by the Tennessee, Buffalo, and Duck Rivers

Of interest: Nathan Bedford Forrest State Park (also in Benton County); Sycamore Landing on Kentucky Lake; Tennessee National Wildlife Refuge (Duck River). During the Civil War, Humphreys County furnished more soldiers than it had registered voters.

Humphreys County Seat—Waverly, Tennessee 37185

Jackson County was established in

1801; named for Andrew Jackson (1767–1845), seventh president of the United States, member of the first State Constitutional Convention, U.S. congressman, senator, major general, veteran of the Creek War and hero of the War of 1812. Gainesboro was named for General Edmund P. Gaines, veteran of the War of 1812.

The first court met in the log home of John Bowen on Roaring River. In 1806 the county seat was established in Williamsburg and in 1817 moved to Gainesboro. A courthouse, built in the 1820s, burned in 1872 and was replaced by a brick courthouse that burned in 1926.

The present courthouse was built in 1927; Tisdale, Pinson, & Stone of Nashville, were the architects.

Census: 1850—15,673 (Whites 14,000; Free Blacks 115; Slaves 1,558); **1950**—12,348; **1990**—9,297 (Whites 9,247; African Americans 7; Native Americans 19; Asians 19; Hispanics 38)

Per capita income (1991): $10,822; 56 percent of the national average

Land area: 309 square miles; drained by the Cumberland River and tributaries

Of interest: Roaring River State Scenic River.

James County occupies a footnote in Tennessee history. The county was established in 1871 from parts of Hamilton and Bradley Counties as a result of the controversy over the location of the Hamilton County seat. Because of insolvency, James County was dissolved in 1919 by the state legislature. The county government ceased to function and was absorbed by Hamilton County in January 1920. James County was named for Jesse J. James by his son, the Honorable E. James, politician and promoter of the new county. *Ooltewah* is an Indian name meaning "Owl Creek."

In its forty-eight-year existence James County had three courthouses. The first two, built in 1874 and in 1890, burned. The third, built in 1913 by W. H. Sears (architect) and W. K. Wilson (contractor), still stands as a monument to a lost cause. The courthouse has at various times served as a Masonic lodge, a sub-police station for Hamilton County, and, more recently, was renovated and used by the Walden Corporation. It is now being used as a public health facility (1994).

> **Census: 1910**—approximately 5000
>
> **Land area:** 255 square miles; drained by the Tennessee River

Jefferson County, first named

Caswell County, was established in 1792 and named for Thomas Jefferson, third president of the United States and principal author of the Declaration of Independence. Dandridge was named for Martha Dandridge Custis, wife of George Washington.

The first courthouse of logs, later known as the Bill Blue Cabin, was not torn down until 1955. A brick courthouse was built in 1796 and was replaced in 1845 by the present courthouse. Construction by Hickman Brothers cost $6,666. The courthouse served as a hospital during the Civil War. Restoration in 1982 sandblasted the brick facing to its original state. The Jefferson County Courthouse is on the National Register of Historic Places.

Census: 1850—13,204 (Whites 11,458; Free Blacks 118; Slaves 1,628); **1950**—19,667; **1990**—33,016 (Whites 31,937; African Americans 930; Native Americans 75; Asians 41; Hispanics 100)

Per capita income (1991): $13,511; 70 percent of the national average

Land area: 274 square miles; drained by the Cumberland River and tributaries

Of interest: Carson-Newman College; Cherokee Lake; Douglas Lake.

Johnson County, first named Wayne County, was established in 1836; named for

Thomas Johnson, an early settler on the Doe River. The county seat, first called Taylorsville in honor of pioneer settler Nathaniel Taylor, was renamed Mountain City in 1885.

The first courthouse was a two-story, 40-foot square building that lasted until 1894 when, declared unsafe, it was torn down. The second courthouse lasted until 1958 when the present courthouse was built by Bo Kenfoot at a cost of $225,000.

In the 1930s, Johnson County became famous as the Green Bean Capital, producing 175 bushels of beans per acre.

An unusual collection of presidential campaign buttons was assembled by County Trustee Jack Reece.

Census: 1850—3,705 (Whites 3,485; Free Blacks 14; Slaves 206); **1950**—12,278; **1990**—13,766 (Whites 13,668; African Americans 61; Native Americans 14; Asians 14; Hispanics 32)

Per capita income (1991): $10,347; 54 percent of the national average

Land area: 299 square miles; drained by the Watauga and Doe Rivers

Of interest: Appalachian Trail; Backbone Rock and tunnel; Cherokee National Forest; Gentry Creek Falls; Old Mill Music Park at Laurel Bloomery; Wautauga Lake.

Johnson County Seat—Mountain City, Tennessee 37683

 **Knox County** was established in 1792; named for Major General Henry Knox, secretary of war in George Washington's cabinet. Knoxville, founded in 1791 on the site of White's Fort, was the first capital of the state of Tennessee from 1796–1811, and again from 1817–1818.

Knox County has had four courthouses. The first, built in 1794, lasted until circa 1813; the second, until 1841. Though the cost of the third courthouse built in 1842 was "not to exceed $10,000," an additional $400 was spent on a dome and clock. Barnes Crawford was the builder. This courthouse was used by both Confederate and Federal troops during the Civil War. The fourth courthouse, built in 1885 by Stephenson & Getaz of Knoxville and described as "an interesting example of a provincial structure designed by a local firm," is on the National Register of Historic Places. This building underwent major renovation in 1988–1989 and became an adjunct to the new City County Building.

A magnificent modern complex, the City County Building, was completed in 1979 and contains an auditorium, a great concourse with balconies, courtrooms, meeting rooms, county and city offices, and the county jail. Designed and built by the City County Building Associated Architects (formed by the architectural firms of Lindsay & Maples and McCarty, Holsaple & McCarty), the facility contains 560,000 square feet and cost approximately $25,000,000. Sixty-four percent of the building, including the jail, is used by the county.

On the grounds of the courthouse are the graves of John Sevier and his two wives, a statue honoring veterans of the Spanish-American War, and a memorial gate to Dr. John Mason Boyd, "our beloved physician" and the first surgeon to successfully perform an hysterectomy.

Census: 1850—18,807 (Whites 16,385; Free Blacks 229; Slaves 2,193); **1950**—223,007; **1990**—335,749 (Whites 301,421; African Americans 29,603; Native Americans 797; Asians 3,327; Hispanics 2,067)

Per capita income (1991): $17,937; 94 percent of the national average

Land area: 509 square miles; drained by the Tennessee, Holston, and Clinch Rivers

National Historic Landmark: William Blount Mansion

Colleges: Knoxville College; University of Tennessee at Knoxville

Of interest: Chilhowee Park; Confederate Memorial Hall; Dulin Art Gallery; Ijams Nature Park; John Sevier's home; Knoxville Zoological Park; Spring Dogwood Festival; General James White's Fort. Governor John Sevier (1745–1815), Democrat, served as the first governor, 1796–1801, and again 1803–1809; Governor Archibald Roane (1759–1819), Democrat, served 1801–1803; Governor William G. "Parson" Brownlow (1805–1887), Republican/Whig, served 1865–1869.

Lake County was established in 1870 and named in honor of Reelfoot Lake

which formed when land movements during the earthquake of 1811 dammed Reelfoot River changing the course of the Mississippi River. The lake is about eighteen miles long, three-quarters of a mile to three miles wide, and some ten feet deep.

Tiptonville, the county seat, was named for William Tipton. Reelfoot is said to be the name of a Chickasaw Indian chief who reeled because of a club foot deformity.

The first county court met in the Athenaeum Hall until the courthouse was built in 1904. This clapboard building was renovated and encased in brick in 1935. The flagpole is the mast of a ship and commemorates the Civil War naval battle at Island No. 10 in the Mississippi River.

Census: 1870—2,428; **1950**—11,656; **1990**—7,129 (Whites 5,418; African Americans 1,702; Native Americans 4; Asians 2; Hispanics 27)

Per capita income (1991): $11,186; 58 percent of the national average

Land area: 163 square miles; bordered by the Mississippi River

Of interest: Lake Isam National Wildlife Refuge; Reelfoot Lake State Park. Clifton B. Cate, Commandant of the U.S. Marine Corps, 1948–1952, was from Lake County.

Lake County Seat—Tiptonville, Tennessee 38079

Lauderdale County was established in 1835; named for Colonel James Lauderdale who was killed in 1814 in the Battle of New Orleans. The county seat was named for General Eleazar Wheelock Ripley, veteran of the War of 1812. Ripley's charter, granted by the legislature in 1901, describes the location . . . "thence north 85 degrees east to a blackgum marked with a cross and with mistletoe on the top and with a bluebird sitting on a limb." Land for the town was purchased from Thomas Brown for $50; lots were sold to raise money for public buildings.

A courthouse, 22 by 26 feet of "good hewed yellow poplar logs," costing $200 was used from 1838 to 1844. Next was a frame building located on the public square and costing $4000, burned in 1869. The third courthouse, built of brick and costing $20,000, served from 1870 to 1936 when it was demolished. The present courthouse, funded in part by the Federal Emergency Administration of Public Works, was built in 1936 for $120,000. Marr & Holman were the architects; R. M. Condra Company, builder. The Lauderdale County Courthouse is on the National Register of Historic Places.

Census: 1850—5,169 (Whites 3,397; Free Blacks 6; Slaves 1,766); 1950—25,047; 1990—23,491 (Whites 16,007; African Americans 7,303; Native Americans 127; Asians 20; Hispanics 178)

Per capita income (1991): $12,662; 66 percent of the national average

Land area: 471 square miles; borders on the Mississippi River

National Historic Landmark: Fort Pillow State Historical Area, 1,646 acres

Of interest: The late Alex Haley, the author of *Roots*, was from Henning.

Lauderdale County Seat—Ripley, Tennessee 38063

 ***Lawrence County*** was established in 1817; named for Captain James Lawrence, the commander of the *Chesapeake* in her fight with the frigate *Shannon* in the War of 1812, who, mortally wounded, gave his famous last command, "Don't give up the ship." David Crockett, among the first settlers in Lawrence County and builder of an extensive installation with dam, grist mill, powder mill, and distillery, was involved in a dispute as to the location of the county seat which was finally placed in Lawrenceburg in 1821. The area was the scene of intense fighting between various Indian tribes and the settlers.

The first log courthouse, located in Jonesboro, was built by Josephus Irvine for $25. A twenty-five-foot square, brick, two-story courthouse, built in Lawrenceburg in 1821 and known as the "David Crockett Courthouse," was taken down in 1905. The third courthouse, erected in 1905 in the town square, had a cupola.

In 1974 the present courthouse was built in a new location for $1,000,000. Hart, Freeland & Roberts of Nashville were the architects.

Census: 1850—9,280 (Whites 8,094; Free Blacks 24; Slaves 1,162); **1950**—28,818; **1990**—35,303 (Whites 34,666 African Americans 482; Native Americans 59; Asians 73; Hispanics 145)

Per capita income (1991): $13,747; 72 percent of the national average

Land area: 617 square miles; drained by tributaries of the Tennessee River

Of interest: Amish Community; David Crockett State Park, 1000 acres; Natchez Trace Parkway (see Hickman County).

 **Lewis County** was established in 1843; named for Captain Meriwether Lewis, co-commander of the Lewis and Clark Expedition to the Pacific Northwest. The county seat was in Gordon and then Newburgh before moving to Hohenwald in 1897. *Hohenwald*, meaning "high forest," was named by a colony of enterprising Swiss settlers.

Because of sparse population, the county was dissolved in 1869 but was reestablished by the legislature ten months later.

The first courthouse (1897) was replaced in 1939 by a courthouse funded by the Federal Emergency Administration of Public Works; Nile Yearwood of Nashville, contractor. The county jail is located on the top floor.

The Farm, a "hippie" utopian commune which at its height had some 1,700 members, was established in 1971 near Summertown under the leadership of Stephen Gaskin of California. By 1994, the commune had evolved into a cooperative of some three hundred members.

Census: 1850—4,438 (Whites 3,694; Free Blacks 8; Slaves 736); 1950—6,078; 1990—9,247 (Whites 9,082; African Americans 119; Native Americans 26; Asians 7; Hispanics 54)

Per capita income (1991): $10,714; 56 percent of the national average

Land area: 282 square miles; drained by tributaries of the Tennessee River

Of interest: Lewis State Forest; Meriwether Lewis National Monument; Natchez Trace Parkway (see Hickman County).

 *Lincoln County* was established in 1809; named for Major General Benjamin Lincoln, veteran of the Revolutionary War. Fayetteville's name honors Marquis de LaFayette (see Fayette County).

The first courthouse, for temporary use only, was built of logs by James Fuller in 1810 at a cost of $35. The second courthouse, a two-story brick building constructed in 1811 by Micajah and William McElroy for $4,745, was used until 1873. The third courthouse, built in 1873 by William T. Moyers, James N. Albright, and William E. Turley, cost $29,579.30. The present courthouse, costing $815,000, was built in 1971–1972. Morton-Carter & Associates of Nashville were the architects; Shepherd Construction Company of Nashville, the contractor. The courthouse is patterned after Independence Hall in Philadelphia.

Census: 1850—23,492 (Whites 17,802; Free Blacks 69; Slaves 5,621); **1950**—25,624; **1990**—28,157 (Whites 25,583; African Americans 2,422; Native Americans 38; Asians 64; Hispanics 137)

Per capita income (1991): $14,041; 73 percent of the national average

Land area: 570 square miles; drained by the Elk River

Of interest: Lincoln Lake.

Lincoln County Seat—Fayetteville, Tennessee 37334

Loudon County, first named Christiana County, was established in 1870, and named in honor of the old British Fort Loudoun which was built in 1756 and named for the Earl of Loudoun (British spelling), commander-in-chief in the southern colonies during the French and Indian Wars.

The courthouse is the original one built in 1872 for $7000. Alexander C. Bruce was the architect; Eli Clarke and his son J. Wesley Clarke, the builders. The Loudon County Courthouse is on the National Register of Historic Places.

East Tennessee was a frontier battleground between the Indians and settlers, especially during the French and Indian War. Remnants of forts and of Indian settlements abound in the region. The site of Tanasi, the Cherokee capital from which Tennessee derived its name, lies under the waters of Tellico Lake.

Census: 1880—9,148; **1950**—23,182; **1990**—31,255 (Whites 30,732; African Americans 400; Native Americans 52; Asians 50; Hispanics 83)

Per capita income (1991): $14,913; 78 percent of the national average

Land area: 229 square miles; drained by the Tennessee and the Little Tennessee Rivers

Of interest: Carmichael Inn (Loudon County Museum); Fort Loudoun Dam and Lake; Tellico Dam and Lake; Tennessee Valley Winery & Loudon Valley Winery.

Macon County was established in

1842; named for Nathanael Macon of North Carolina, Revolutionary War veteran, speaker of the U.S. House of Representatives, and U.S. senator. Lafayette was named in honor of Marquis de LaFayette (see Fayette County).

There have been four courthouses in Macon County; three burned, thought by some to have occurred "just before an audit of the county records was to take place." Most records prior to 1901 have been destroyed. The first courthouse, built in 1844 for $4000 by Britton Holland and Thomas A. Williams, burned in 1860. The second courthouse, built by Robert Allen and Charles Carter for $10,000, burned in 1901. The third courthouse, built by a contractor named Yeaman for $10,800, burned in 1932. The fourth and present courthouse was completed in 1933 for $16,600 by L. E. Tate & Son of Nashville; renovations took place in the early 1970s.

Census: 1850—6,948 (Whites 6,122; Free Blacks 60; Slaves 766); **1950**—13,599; **1990**—16,146 (Whites 15,810; African Americans 44; Native Americans 35; Asians 10; Hispanics 39)

Per capita income (1991): $11,979; 62 percent of the national average

Land area: 307 square miles; drained by the tributaries of the Cumberland and Big Barren Rivers

Of interest: The Donoho Hotel at Red Boiling Springs, nineteenth-century health spa famous for its mineral waters, is located six miles south of Bug Tussle, Tennessee.

Madison County was established in 1821; named in honor of James Madison, fourth president of the United States. The county seat was named for President Andrew Jackson.

A 30- by 40-foot log courthouse was built by John Houston for $135. In 1824 a two-story brick courthouse was built by Benjamin Gholson. In 1839 a more substantial courthouse, 50 by 60 feet, was built for $25,000 by Thomas Brown, contractor. This courthouse was remodeled in 1848 and used until 1907. During the Civil War, the bell from the courthouse tower was donated to General Pierre Gustave Toutant de Beauregard and melted into bullets. The current courthouse, partly funded by the Federal Emergency Administration of Public Works, was built for $300,000 in 1936. The exterior is of Indiana limestone while Tennessee marble was used inside. Marr & Holman of Nashville, were the architects; Foster & Creighton Company, the contractors. The Madison Court-

house is on the National Register of Historic Places.

Census: 1850—21,470 (Whites 12,857; Free Blacks 61; Slaves 8,552); 1950—60,128; 1990—77,982 (Whites 53,423; African Americans 24,170; Native Americans 66; Asians 253; Hispanics 376)

Per capita income (1991): $16,101; 84 percent of the national average

Land area: 557 square miles; drained by the Forked Deer River

National Historic Landmark: Pinson Mounds State Archaeological Area

Colleges: Lambuth College; Lane College; Union University

Of interest: Casey Jones Home and Railroad Museum.

Marion County was established in 1817; named for Brigadier General Francis Marion, the "Swamp Fox" of Revolutionary War fame. The county seat, named for Sergeant William Jasper, Revolutionary War hero, was built on land deeded to the county in 1823 for one dollar by Betsy Pack, an Indian.

Prior to 1823 the county courts met in Whitwell in the Cheek home, a double-log house. The first courthouse in Jasper, a brick building constructed by John Mathas, was used from 1824 to 1879. A larger courthouse, built by John Jones in 1880, burned in 1922. The origin of this fire was never determined, and many records were lost.

The present courthouse was completed in 1925 and burned April 2, 1983. Renovation was completed in 1986.

Census: 1850—6,314 (Whites 5,718; Free Blacks 45; Slaves 551); **1950**—20,520; **1990**—24,860 (Whites 23,749; African Americans 1,035; Native Americans 36; Asians 32; Hispanics 85)

Per capita income (1991): $12,509; 65 percent of the national average

Land area: 500 square miles; drained by the Sequatchie and Tennessee Rivers

Of interest: Guntersville Lake; Grundy Forest State Natural Area; Franklin State Forest; Nickajack Lake; Prentice Cooper State Forest. Governor Peter Turney (1827–1903), Democrat, served 1893–1897.

70

Marion County Seat—Jasper, Tennessee 37347

 *Marshall County* was established in 1836; named for John Marshall, U.S. congressman, secretary of state, and chief justice 1801–1835. Lewisburg was named in honor of Meriwether Lewis, explorer of the Pacific Northwest.

Marshall County has had three courthouses. The first, built in 1836 of brick fired on the square, was a two-story building topped with a cupola, cost $8,750, and was destroyed by fire in 1872. The second brick courthouse with clock tower was erected in 1874, cost $21,000, and burned in 1927. The present courthouse, completed in 1929 at a cost of $125,000, was remodeled in 1974 for $377,407.69. Hart, Freeland & Roberts of Nashville were the architects in 1929 and in 1974. James Knox Polk practiced law in Lewisburg from 1841 until his election as president of the United States in 1844.

Census: 1850—15,616 (Whites 11,915; Free Blacks 67; Slaves 3,634); **1950**—17,768; **1990**—21,539 (Whites 19,536; African Americans 1,909; Native Americans 24; Asians 53; Hispanics 92)

Per capita income (1991): $14,816; 77 percent of the national average

Land area: 375 square miles; drained by the Duck River

Of interest: Henry Horton State Resort Park. Governor Henry H. Horton (1866–1934), Democrat, served 1927–1933; Governor Jim Nance McCord (1879–1968), Democrat, served 1945–1949; Governor Buford Ellington (1907–1972), Democrat, served 1959–1963 and 1969–1971.

Marshall County Seat—Lewisburg,, Tennessee 37091   71

 *Maury County* was established in 1807; named for Abram Maury of Williamson County who surveyed and laid out the counties of West Tennessee. He was state senator in 1805 and also served in the state house of representatives. Columbia was named for Christopher Columbus.

Maury County has had four courthouses. The first, a log building, was occupied in 1808. A brick courthouse was completed in 1811 for $6,900 by Goodloe & Nicholson, contractors. James Knox Polk, as a member of the Maury County Bar, argued cases in this building; President Martin Van Buren visited in 1842. The third courthouse was completed in 1847 at the cost of $19,170. William Watkins drew the plans; Nimrod Porter was the contractor. During the Civil War the courthouse, occupied by both Federal and Confederate troops, was badly damaged.

The present courthouse, its tower 132 feet above the street, was built in 1906 for $120,000 and is on the National Register of Historic Places. The architectural firm of Carpenter & Blair of New York prepared plans which were considered to be a "Gift to Posterity." The contract went to Hugger Brothers. The cornerstone, laid with appropriate ceremony in 1904, was filled with mementos from the past. Extensive renovations were carried out in 1972–1973 at the cost of $236,000. Howard, Nielson, Lyne, Batey, and O'Brien, Inc. were the architects; L. E. Kirk & Son, the contractor. The Maury County records are complete.

Census: 1850—29,520 (Whites 16,759; Free blacks 91; Slaves 12,670); **1950**—40,368; **1990**—54,812 (Whites 45,868; African Americans 8,607; Native Americans 79; Asians 157; Hispanics 323)

Per capita income (1991): $18,188; 95 percent of the national average

Land area: 613 square miles; drained by the Duck River

National Landmarks: James K. Polk House; Rattle and Snap Plantation

Of interest: Athenaeum; Mt. Pleasant, "Phosphate Capital of the World"; Natchez Trace Parkway; St. John's Episcopal Church; Zion Presbyterian Church. Columbia is known as the "Mule Capital of the World." Maury County has many well-preserved antebellum homes. President James Knox Polk (1795–1849) was the eleventh president of the United States (1845–1849) and served as governor of Tennessee (1839–1841). Maury County was his boyhood home.

McMinn County was established

in 1819; named for Joseph McMinn, then governor of Tennessee. The county seat was Calhoun from 1819 to 1823 when it moved to Athens, named for the historic Greek capital.

From 1823, the county used existing buildings until a two-story brick courthouse, 40 by 46 feet, was built in 1828. A second "grand" courthouse was built in 1875 costing $30,000. A. C. Bruce of Knoxville was the architect; Thomas and W. C. Cleage, contractors. This building burned in November of 1964 as it was being renovated. The present courthouse was built in 1967 for $750,000. Galloway & Guthrie of Knoxville were the architects; Webb Brothers of Athens, the contractors.

Census: 1850—13,906 (Whites 12,286; Free Blacks 52; Slaves 1,568); **1950**—32,024; **1990**—42,383 (Whites 40,085; African Americans 2,051; Native Americans 96; Asians 121; Hispanics 174)

Per capita income (1991): $13,764; 72 percent of the national average

Land area: 430 square miles; drained by the Hiwassee River

Colleges: Tennessee Wesleyan College

Of interest: Cherokee National Forest; Chickamauga Lake; Etowah, Indian Village mounds; Museums—Globe Swift, Living Heritage, Englewood Textile; 1854 Niota Depot. Governor Joseph McMinn (1758–1824), Democrat, served 1815–1821; Governor DeWitt Clinton Senter (1830–1898), Republican/Whig, served 1869–1871.

McMinn County Seat—Athens, Tennessee 37303

 **McNairy County** was estab-
lished in 1823; named for Judge John McNairy
who, appointed by George Washington to the Superior Court of the
Western District of North Carolina, arrived in Nashville in 1788. The
county seat, originally established in Purdy in 1825, moved to Selmer
in 1890 when Purdy was bypassed by the railroad.

The first court in Purdy was held in the log cabin home of Abel V. Murray. U.S. Congressman David Crockett delivered the opening speech at the new 1830 courthouse built in Purdy. Henry Kirkland was the contractor; James Reed, the builder. This courthouse burned in 1881.

Selmer has had two courthouses. The first, built in 1891, was presented to the county by P. H. Thrasher in order to facilitate the move from Purdy. The present courthouse was erected in 1948; Marr & Holman of Nashville, architects. In 1903 a statue honoring the early settlers was placed on the grounds.

Census: 1850—12,864 (Whites 11,447; Free Blacks 24; Slaves 1,393); **1950**—20,300; **1990**—22,422 (Whites 20,918 African Americans 1,432; Native Americans 21; Asians 40, Hispanics 95)

Per capita income (1991): $12,895; 67 percent of the national average

Land area: 560 square miles; drained by the Hatchie River

Of interest: Big Hill Pond State Park. Sheriff Buford Pusser, the crime-fighting hero of the movie *Walking Tall*, was from McNairy County.

 ***Meigs County*** was established in 1836; named in honor of Return Jonathan Meigs, a colonel in the Revolutionary War who fought at the Battle of Lexington and at Quebec, Sag Harbor, and Stony Point. He served as Indian agent for the Cherokee from 1801 until his death in 1823. Decatur was named for Commodore Stephen Decatur (see Decatur County).

Meigs County has had three courthouses. The first was built in 1837 for $2,400. The second, built in 1882, was burned in 1902. The present courthouse, designed by W. R. Harper and built by Broadway Manufacturing of Knoxville, was built in 1904 for approximately $7,645. The bricks were handmade on the site. The Meigs County Courthouse is on the National Register of Historic Places.

Tradition has it that Sam Houston, who was adopted by Chief Jolly of the Cherokee Nation, spent time at the chief's home on Jolly's Island at the mouth of the Hiwassee River where he was given the name "The Raven." Chief Jolly's Cherokee name *Olooteca* means "He Who Puts the Drum Away" signifying his desire for peace in an area devastated by warfare between Indians and settlers.

John Walker Jr., grandson of Nancy Ward, the "Beloved Woman" of the Cherokees who warned the settlers of Cherokee attacks, married Emily Meigs, a relative of Return Jonathan Meigs. In the 1830s Walker supported the Treaty Party which advocated the movement of the Indians to the West.

Census: 1850—4,879 (Whites 4,480; Free Blacks 4; Slaves 395); **1950**—6,080; **1990**—8,033 (Whites 7,884; African Americans 118; Native Americans 28; Asians 2; Hispanics 17)

Per capita income (1991): $12,682; 66 percent of the national average

Land area: 195 square miles; drained by the Hiwassee and the Tennessee Rivers

Of interest: Blythe Ferry and Washington Ferry (toll ferries) on the Tennessee River; Chicamauga Lake; Watts Bar Lake.

Monroe County was established in 1819; named for James Monroe, fifth president of the United States. The county seat was named Tellico until 1830 when it was changed to Madisonville in honor of James Madison, the fourth president of the United States.

The first courthouse, built around 1825, burned in 1832. The second, built of brick in 1835, was burned by the Yankees in 1864 and was replaced in 1868 by a two-story brick building. The present courthouse was built in 1897. Bauman Brothers were the architects; Galyon Seldon Company, the contractors. Extensive renovations, including an annex, were carried out in 1979. The Monroe County Courthouse is on the National Register of Historic Places.

Monroe County is birthplace of Sequoya, leader of the Cherokee Nation. He invented the Cherokee written language which was made up of eighty-five symbols in the alphabet.

Census: 1850—11,874 (Whites 10,623; Free Blacks 63; Slaves 1,188); **1950**—24,513; **1990**—30,541 (Whites 29,561; African Americans 833; Native Americans 48; Asians 71; Hispanics 123)

Per capita income (1991): $12,017; 63 percent of the national average

Land area: 635 square miles; drained by the Tellico and Little Tennessee Rivers

National Historic Landmark: Fort Loudoun State Historical Area

Of interest: Calderwood Reservoir; Cherokee National Forest; Chota & Tansai Cherokee Villages Sites; Lost Sea, underground lake; Tellico Blockhouse; Tellico Wildlife Management Area; Toqua Village Site. Estes Kefauver (1903–1963) U.S. senator, congressman, statesman, was vice presidential nominee for the Democratic party in 1956.

Montgomery County was established in 1796; named for Colonel John Montgomery who, with Martin Armstrong, founded Clarksville. Montgomery, an explorer, Revolutionary War hero, and Indian fighter, was killed by Indians in 1794. Clarksville was named for George Rogers Clark, explorer and Revolutionary War hero.

Montgomery County has had four courthouses. The first was a log structure built around 1796 by James Adams on the public square and was replaced in 1811 by a two-story brick building built by Colemore Duvall. The third, built in 1842 on Franklin Street, burned in 1878 and was replaced by the present courthouse at an overall cost of $100,000. S. W. Bunting and C. G. Rosenplaenter were the architects; McCormack & Sweeney, the builders. This courthouse was considered one of the "handsomest buildings in the South" and is part of the Clarksville Architectural District on the National Register of Historic Places. The interior of the courthouse burned in 1900, and was promptly restored. Further renovations were carried out in 1966 and again in 1976.

Monuments on the courthouse lawn memorialize Valentine Sevier and other pioneers killed by Indians; honors those who made the ultimate sacrifice for our country in World Wars I and II, the Korean War, and Vietnam; and commemorates Governor Austin Peay.

Census: 1850—21,045 (Whites 11,900; Free Blacks 74; Slaves 9,071); **1950**—44,186; **1990**—100,498 (Whites 79,118; African Americans 17,872; Native Americans 394; Asians 1,831; Hispanics 3,228)

Per capita income (1991): $13,736; 72 percent of the national average

Land area: 539 square miles; drained by the Red and the Cumberland Rivers

Of interest: Austin Peay State University; Clarksville-Montgomery County Museum; Fort Defiance/Fort Bruce; Fort Campbell Military Reservation; Port Royal Covered Bridge and state historical area. Dunbar State Cave, archaeological area purchased in 1948 by the "King of Country Music" Roy Acuff, was a popular site for square dances and country music broadcasts; in 1973 it became a state natural area. The late Wilma Rudolph, a native of Clarksville, won three gold medals in Olympic track competition in Rome in 1961. Governor William Blount (1768–1835), Democrat, served 1809–1815; Governor Austin Peay (1876–1927), Democrat, served 1923–1927.

Moore County was established in 1871; named for Major General William Moore, veteran of the Creek War and the War of 1812. Tradition has it that, in the early days, vigilantes maintained law and order, and offenses were punished at the whipping post. A small weakly man named Lynch administered the lash; hence the place was called Lynchburg.

The courthouse was built in 1885. Prior to that date court was held in Tolley and Eaton's Hall (known as the Old Red Hall), in the Christian Church until it burned in 1883, and in the schoolhouse. The courthouse was built by S. L. P. Garrett for $6,875 and is on the National Register of Historic Places. The walls, twenty inches thick of brick fired in Lynchburg, are held together with sand and lime. Renovation was carried out in 1967–1968 with funds contributed in part by the Jack Daniel Distillery Company. Frank Hise of Lynchburg, contractor, was able to find matching brick in Shelbyville and foundation rock in Fayetteville so that the enlarged building retains its original charm.

Census: 1880—6,233; 1950—3,948; 1990—4,721 (Whites 4,536; African Americans 174; Native Americans 8; Asians 2; Hispanics 20)

Per capita income (1991): $10,998; 57 percent of the national average

Land area: 129 square miles; drained by the Elk River

Of interest: Jack Daniel Distillery Museum; Restored Lynchburg, a popular tourist attraction

Moore County remained "dry" until 1994 even though its main industry is the popular whiskey produced by the Jack Daniel Distillery.

Morgan County was established in 1817; named in honor of Brigadier General Daniel Morgan, Revolutionary War veteran. The first county seat in 1817 was Montgomery, named for a surveyor in the area. A second county seat, also called Montgomery, was set up on the Emory River one mile west of Wartburg where the first courthouse was built in 1826. Wartburg was named by German settlers for the castle where Martin Luther began his German translation of the New Testament.

In 1870 the county seat moved to Wartburg where a two-story frame courthouse was built for $3,132 by A. J. Hurtt, J. Kreis, D. Kreis. In 1904 the present brick courthouse was built for $14,500 on land donated by George Frederick Gerding. W. Chamberlin & Co., architects; W. R. Harper, contractor. A wing was added in 1959. Morton & Sweetser, architects; Emory & Richards, contractors. Renovation, in 1978, was by Barge, Waggoner, Sumner & Cannon, architects; Vickers Construction Company, contractor.

Census: 1850—3,430 (Whites 3,301; Free Blacks 28; Slaves 101); **1950**—15,727; **1990**—17,300 (Whites 16,957; African Americans 265; Native Americans 46; Asians 25; Hispanics 60)

Per capita income (1991): $11,046; 58 percent of the national average

Land area: 522 square miles; drained by the Emory and Obed Rivers

Of interest: Big South Fork National River & Recreational Area, 10,000 acres; Catoosa Wildlife Management Area; Lone Mountain State Forest, 3,597 acres; Mount Roosevelt State Forest (also in Roane County); Rugby (also in Scott County).

Morgan County Seat—Wartburg, Tennessee 37887

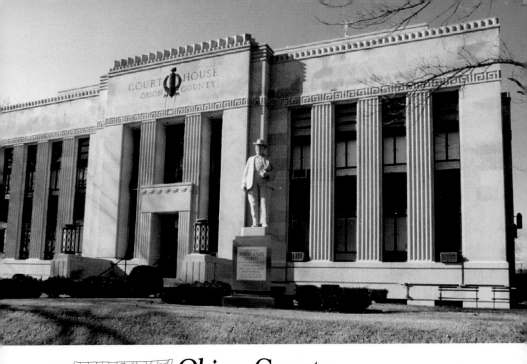

Obion County was established in

1823; named for the Obion River. The county seat was located in Troy (1823–1890) and moved to Union City when the building of the railroad caused a shift in population and power.

Three courthouses were erected in Troy. The first, a log structure built in 1825, was replaced in 1831 by a two-story brick building fifty-foot square which was damaged by a severe earthquake in 1842. A third courthouse was built in 1852. Union City has had two courthouses. The present courthouse was partly funded in 1939 by the Federal Emergency Administration of Public Works at a cost of $200,000. Marr & Holman were the architects; F. C. Gorrell & Sons, the builders. The Obion County Courthouse is on the National Register of Historic Places.

Census: 1850—7,663 (Whites 6,572; Free Blacks 4; Slaves 1,057); **1950**—29,056; **1990**—31,717 (Whites 28,324; African Americans 3,256; Native Americans 47; Asians 48; Hispanics 138)

Per capita income (1991): $14,579; 76 percent of the national average

Land area: 545 square miles; drained by the Obion River

Of interest: Gooch Waterfowl Management Area; Obion County Museum; Reelfoot Lake State Park and National Wildlife Refuge (see Lake County). A monument to the late Congressman Robert A. "Fats" Everett is inscribed with his famous maxim, "If a man don't want to work, he hadn't ought to hire out." The famous trial of the "Night Riders of Reelfoot Lake" took place in the courthouse in Union City in 1909.

Overton County was established in

1806; named in honor of Judge John Overton, co-founder of the city of Memphis. Livingston was named for Edgar Livingston, secretary of state in President Andrew Jackson's cabinet.

The first courthouse was built of logs in Monroe in 1808. In 1835 a vote was cast to move the county seat to Livingston; Livingston won by four votes. It is said that "Ranter" Eldridge, a farmer from Nettle Carrier, left his home with six men committed to Monroe. They spent the night at an inn. Early the next morning, "Ranter" arose before his opponents and turned their horses loose. Had these men been able to vote, Monroe would have remained the county seat of Overton. A courthouse, built in Livingston in 1835 and enlarged in 1850, was burned by Civil War raiders. The present courthouse, built in 1868–1869 by "Little" Joe Copeland for $9,999.99, is on the National Register of Historic Places.

It was remodeled in 1979 by Thomas & Miller, architects; Jacobs Construction Co., contractors.

Census: 1850—11,211 (Whites 10,088; Free Blacks 58; Slaves 1,065); **1950**—17,566; **1990**—17,636 (Whites 17,582; African Americans 30; Native Americans 10; Asians 4; Hispanics 73)

Per capita income (1991): $10,055; 52 percent of the national average

Land area: 433 square miles; drained by the Obey and Roaring Rivers

Of interest: Scenic Roaring River; Standing Stone State Park (11,000 acres); Wilder Coal Mine Wilderness Area. Governor Albert Houston Roberts (1868–1946), Democrat, served 1919–1921.

Perry County was established in 1819; named for Commodore Oliver Hazard Perry who served in the naval battle in Tripoli and in the Battle of Lake Erie (1813) where he sent his famous message, "We have met the enemy, and they are ours." The county seat was in Perryville (on the west bank of the Tennessee River) until 1846 when Decatur County was established. It was then moved to Harrisburg for two years and, with a majority of only six votes, moved to Linden in 1848. Linden was named for the many linden trees in the area.

A temporary building of logs served as the courthouse until 1849 when a frame building was put up. This courthouse burned during the Civil War (1863) with many records lost. A two-story brick courthouse, built in 1868 for $9500, burned as it was being renovated in January 1928. The present courthouse was completed in 1928 for $47,000 and is on the National Register of Historic Places. C. K. Colley of Nashville was the architect; Bell Brothers, the contractor.

Census: 1850—5,821 (Whites 5,503; Free Blacks 5; Slaves 313); **1950**—5,462; **1990**—6,612 (Whites 6,470; African Americans 119; Native Americans 8; Asians 7; Hispanics 36)

Per capita income (1991): $12,177: 64 percent of the national average

Land area: 415 square miles; drained by the Buffalo and the Tennessee Rivers

Of interest: Canoeing on the Buffalo River; Kentucky Lake; Mousetail Landing State Rustic Park.

Perry County Seat—Linden, Tennessee 37096

Pickett County was established in

1879; named for Howell L. Pickett, state representative from Wilson County. The county seat was named for Colonel Robert Byrd of Kingston.

The first courthouse was built in 1881 by Tom Ray, Tom Babb, Buchanan Matheny, and Pharoah Morgan. Morgan boasted that he made more money one night than in any one day of his life by driving the stakes for the foundation down one foot.

The present courthouse was built in 1935 of mountain stone quarried nearby. Marr & Holman were the architect; Nile Yearwood was the contractor. The Pickett County Courthouse is on the National Register of Historic Places.

Census: 1890—4,718; 1950—5,093; 1990—4,548 (Whites 4,542; African Americans 0; Native Americans 4; Asians 2; Hispanics 13); Pickett County has the smallest population of any county in the state

Per capita income (1991): $9,368; 49 percent of the national average

Land area: 163 square miles; drained by the Obey and Wolf Rivers

Of interest: Cordell Hull (secretary of state under President F. D. Roosevelt during World War II) birthplace and museum; Dale Hollow Lake; Pickett State Rustic Park (1000 acres).

Polk County was established in 1839; named for James Knox Polk, eleventh president of the United States. During his presidency, he conducted the Mexican War and enlarged the United States by some 500,000 square miles including Texas, California, and most of the southwest. In 1845 President Polk introduced the use of the postage stamp for prepayment of postage. The county seat was named for Thomas Hart Benton, U.S. senator for thirty years.

Polk County has had four courthouses. The first, completed in 1840, was a wooden building 30 by 20 feet with two doors and two windows. The second courthouse, a two-story brick building constructed in 1846, burned in 1895. The third courthouse, built in 1897 for $9000, was destroyed by fire in 1936. The present courthouse, funded in part by the Federal Emergency Administration of Public Works at a cost of $100,000, was built in 1937. R. H. Hunt was architect; Forcum-Jones Company, contractor. Polk County Courthouse is on the National Register of Historic Places.

Census: 1850—6,338 (Whites 5,884; Free Blacks 54; Slaves 400); 1950—11,917; 1990—13,643 (Whites 13,571; African Americans 0; Native Americans 25; Asians 42; Hispanics 36)

Per capita income (1991): $11,217; 59 percent of the national average

Land area: 435 square miles; drained by the Hiwassee and Ocoee Rivers

Of interest: Burra Burra Mine Historic District, Ducktown; Cherokee National Forest; Hiwassee State Scenic River; Ocoee River Recreational Area (whitewater rafting); tomb of Nancy Ward. In 1837 the Cherokee Nation departed from Polk County on the tragic "Trail of Tears."

Polk County Seat—Benton, Tennessee 37307

89

Putnam County was established in 1842, dissolved, and reestablished in 1854; named for Major General Israel Putnam veteran of the French & Indian War and the Revolutionary War. The county seat was named for Major Richard Fielding Cooke who was largely responsible for the 1854 reestablishment of the county.

Putnam County has had three courthouses. The first, a brick structure built in 1856, burned in the Civil War. The second, built in 1866 by David L. Dow, burned in 1898 with all records lost. The present building was built in 1900 at a cost of approximately $30,000. James H. Yeaman was the architect; Scott & Smoot, the contractors. The courthouse was remodeled in 1962 by Wilson & Odom, architects and engineers. The monument on the courthouse grounds honors Jere Whitson (1853–1928) who helped establish Tennessee Technological University on land which he donated.

Census: 1870—8,698; 1950—28,869; 1990—51,373 (Whites 4,878; African Americans 873; Native Americans 79; Asians 457; Hispanics 294)

Per capita income (1991): $15,182; 79 percent of the national average

Land area: 401 square miles; drained by tributaries of the Caney Fork and Cumberland Rivers

Of interest: Burgess Falls State National Area (also in White County); Monterey and Bloomington Springs, nineteenth-century summer resorts; Tennessee Technological University.

Rhea County

Rhea County was established in 1807; named for John Rhea, of Sullivan County, veteran of the Revolutionary War, member of the Tennessee Constitutional Convention, and the Tennessee and U.S. House of Representatives. From 1808 to 1812 courts were held at Big Springs, home of William Henry, until the county seat was established at Washington on the Tennessee River. The county seat was moved to Dayton in 1890 because of its location on the Cincinnati to Chattanooga railroad.

Two courthouses were built in Washington in 1813 and in 1831; the latter damaged, but not destroyed, by a tornado in 1833. The present courthouse was built in 1891. W. Chamberlin & Company of Knoxville were the architects; William Dowling and J. R. Taylor of Chattanooga, builders. In 1978 $1,000,000 was spent on restoration of the courthouse. The Franklin Group were the architects; Vickers Construction Co., contractor. The Rhea County Courthouse, a National Historic Landmark, is on the National Register of Historic Places.

Census: 1850—4,415 (Whites 3,951; Free Blacks 28; Slaves 436); **1950**—16,041; **1990**—24,344 (Whites 23,571; African Americans 581; Native Americans 62; Asians 53; Hispanics 132)

Per capita income (1991): $14,270; 74 percent of the national average

Land area: 316 square miles; borders the Tennessee River

Of interest: Bryan College, named for William Jennings Bryan; Chickamauga Lake; Laurel-Snow State Natural Area; Watts Bar Dam and Lake. On July 10, 1925, Dayton was the site of the famous Scopes "Monkey Trial."

 **Roane County** was established in 1801; named for Judge Archibald Roane, second governor of Tennessee (1801–1803). Kingston was named for Robert King, an early settler who owned the land on which the town was built.

Kingston served as the capital of Tennessee for one day, September 21, 1807. The legislators met and immediately resolved to "adjourn forthwith from Kingston." This brief meeting of the legislature was in technical fulfillment of terms in a treaty with the Cherokees by which the Indians relinquished the site of Southwest Point with the understanding that the capital of the state of Tennessee would be located at Kingston. Some politicians' promises, it might seem, were as trustworthy in 1807 as they are today.

Roane County has had three courthouses. The first, built around 1814, had a "handsome dome or cupola." The second, designed by Frederick B. Guenther and built in 1853–1856 for $9,400 by John D. Lowery and Augustus O. Fisher, is topped by a cupola which, it is said, contains a gallows that was used at least once. The "Old" Roane County Courthouse is on the National Register of Historic Places and houses the Roane County Museum of History and Art. The present courthouse, completed in 1975 at a cost of $1,200,000, was designed by Martin J. Lide, architect, and built by Webb Construction Company of Athens.

Census: 1850—12,185 (Whites 10,525; Free Blacks 116; Slaves 1,544); 1950—31,665; 1990—48,094 (Whites 45,444; African Americans 1,456; Native Americans 95; Asians 191; Hispanics 212)

Per capita income (1991): $16,091; 84 percent of the national average

Land area: 361 square miles; drained by the Tennessee and Clinch Rivers

National Historic Landmark: X-10 Atomic Reactor, Oak Ridge Laboratory

Of interest: Melton Hill Lake; Mt. Roosevelt State Forest (also in Morgan County); Watts Bar Lake. Sam Houston was a clerk in a store in Kingston when he enlisted in the Creek War. Sam Rayburn, "Mr. Sam," speaker of the U.S. House of Representatives from 1940 for seventeen years, was born in Roane County in 1882.

 **Robertson County** was established in 1796; named in honor of James Robertson, the "Father of Middle Tennessee." He was the leader in the Watauga Settlement, explored the Cumberland country, and in 1779 led an expedition to found "Nashborough" which later became Nashville.

Robertson County has had three courthouses. The first, a log building, was built in 1799 and sold in 1819 for $116.55. The second, a two-story brick building costing $6,593, was considered very "modern." However, by 1879 it was considered liable to fall at any time from hard wind and heavy rains and regarded as manifestly unsafe, dangerous, and totally unfit as a receptacle for preservation of public records. The present courthouse, which is on the National Register of Historic Places, was constructed in 1879 for $20,959.40. The architect was William C. Smith; the contractors, Patton & McInturff. In 1929–1930 a clock, tower, and wings were added. The architects were Edward Dougherty and Thomas Gardner. The courthouse was further renovated in 1973 and in 1982.

Census: 1850—16,145 (Whites 11,503; Free Blacks 26; Slaves 4,616); **1950**—27,024; **1990**—41,494 (Whites 36,802; African Americans 4,555; Native Americans 63; Asians 43; Hispanics 173)

Per capita income (1991): $14,149; 74 percent of the national average

Land area: 477 square miles; drained by tributaries of the Cumberland River

Of interest: Robertson County is the home of the so-called "Bell Witch" of Adams about whom many hair-raising stories are told.

Robertson County Seat—Springfield, Tennessee 37172

Rutherford County was established in 1803; named for Major General Griffith Rutherford, veteran of the Revolutionary War and member of the Legislature for the Southwest Territory which later became the state of Tennessee. The county seat was first located in the town of Jefferson (Old Jefferson) on land between the forks of the Stone's River where a two-story brick courthouse was built. The county seat was moved to Murfreesboro in 1811. First named Cannonsburg in honor of Newton Cannon (governor of Tennessee from 1835 to 1839), the name was changed to Murfreesboro in honor of Colonel Hardy Murfree, Revolutionary War hero who had recently died.

Rutherford County has had three courthouses. The first, built in 1812, burned in 1822 while Murfreesboro was the capital of Tennessee (1819–1825). The second courthouse, built of brick, cost $6000. The present courthouse was built in 1859 for $50,000 and is on the National Register of Historic Places. James H. Yeaman was the architect; E. E. Dandridge, builder. This courthouse is one of the seven pre-Civil War courthouses still in use.

In 1862 General Nathan Bedford Forrest captured the courthouse from Federal troops in order to rescue several Confederate prisoners who were about to be hanged. The walls carry marks from the minié balls used in that encounter.

Census: 1850—29,122 (Whites 16,910; Free Blacks 234; Slaves 11,978); **1950**—40,696; **1990**—118,570 (Whites 105,740; African Americans 10,678; Native Americans 234; Asians 1,706; Hispanics 926)

Per capita income (1991): $16,047; 84 percent of the national average

Land area: 619 square miles; drained by the Stone's River

Of interest: Fortress Rosecrans Site, Stones River; Middle Tennessee State University; Stone's River National Battlefield and Cemetery. In the 1920s a "human fly," a daredevil steeplejack who had successfully scaled the Woolworth Building in New York City, made a nocturnal ascent to the pinnacle of the courthouse; on the way down he slipped and fell to his death.

Scott County was established in 1849; named for General Winfield Scott who was a veteran of three wars: the War of 1812, the Mexican War, and the Civil War. The county seat is said to be named for an early hunter named Hunt.

Scott County has had four court-houses. The first, a two-story frame building constructed in 1850–1851, was replaced in the early 1870s by a wooden courthouse. The third, built of native stone in 1906 by a man named Holmes, burned in 1946 with many of the records. The present courthouse was completed in 1948 at a cost of $222,000. Clem H. Myer was the architect; John H. Johnson & Sons, the builder.

In 1861, following a speech by Senator Andrew Johnson (later president), Scott County seceded from the state of Tennessee and declared itself the Free and Independent State of Scott.

Census: 1850—1,905 (Whites 1,868; Free Blacks 0; Slaves 37); **1950**—17,362; **1990**—18,358 (Whites 18,263; African Americans 5; Native Americans 67; Asians 13; Hispanics 38)

Per capita income (1991): $11,569; 60 percent of the national average

Land area: 532 square miles; drained by tributaries of the Cumberland River

Of interest: Big South Fork National River & Recreational Area; Honey Creek State Natural Area; Round Knob Mountain (2,960 feet); Scott State Forest (3,182 acres). Scott County is home to U.S. Senator Howard H. Baker Jr., chief of staff under President Ronald Reagan. Rugby, the utopian colony founded in 1880 by British author Thomas Hughes, was an attempt to provide a self-supporting community for the younger sons of English gentry who failed to inherit ancestral fortunes.

Sequatchie County was established in 1857; named in honor of the Sequatchie River Valley, named for the Cherokee chief who journeyed to Charleston, South Carolina, in the early eighteenth century to sign a treaty with the colonial government. The Indian word *sequatchie* means "opossum, he grins and runs." Dunlap, formerly Coops Creek, was named for William Dunlap of Knoxville to enlist his support for creation of the new county. Dunlap became the county seat in 1858.

The first court met January 1858 in the home of Joel Wheeler in the Walnut Valley Community. Benjamin F. Bridgman brought suit protesting the formation of Sequatchie County from Bledsoe County. Final settlement by the Supreme Court of Tennessee concluded that the suit was without merit. Business of the county was suspended during the Civil War. The present courthouse was built in 1911 for $12,000 by W. K. Brown & Brothers. The Sequatchie Courthouse is on the National Register of Historic Places.

Census: 1870—2,335; 1950—5,685; 1990—8,863 (Whites 8,851; African Americans 2; Native Americans 4; Asians 5; Hispanics 25)

Per capita income (1991): $11,616; 61 percent of the national average

Land area: 266 square miles; drained by the Sequatchie River

Of interest: Celebration of Independence Day with parade, square dancing, and festivities on the courthouse lawn is an annual county tradition.

Sequatchie County Seat—Dunlap, Tennessee 37327

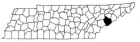 **Sevier County** was established in 1794; named for John Sevier, veteran of thirty-five battles in the Revolutionary and Indian Wars, governor of the state of Franklin, and the first governor of the state of Tennessee (1796–1801) serving a second term 1803–1809. He was elected to three terms as representative to the U.S. Congress. Sevierville was laid out in 1795.

The first court was held in a building that had previously been used as a stable and was infested with fleas. To quote from W. A. Goodspeed, "lawyers accomplished its destruction (by fire) with the assistance of an Irishman with a bottle of whisky."

Sevier County has had five courthouses. The first, of logs, was built circa 1796; the second was a frame building constructed in 1820; the third, built of brick in 1850, burned in 1856 with all records and the death of one person; the fourth, built in 1857, was replaced by the present building in 1895–1896 at the cost of approximately $21,000. The architects were McDonald Brothers; C. W. Brown, the contractor. Much of the material (stone, brick, lumber) was acquired locally. An Italian stonecutter, "said to be blind," did the hand cutting of the stone. A Seth Thomas clock, now on exhibit in the courthouse lobby, originally cost $1,396 and was replaced by an electric clock in 1974. The courthouse was renovated in 1971–1975 for over one million dollars.

In 1992 a three-story annex was added for $1,700,000. Robert Grubb was the architect; Rouse Construction, contractor. In 1993 major restoration of the old courthouse, including remodeling the clock tower and its domes, was carried out for $300,000. Robert Grubb was the architect, and Joseph Construction Co., the builders. A life-size bronze statue of country music star Dolly Parton, with her guitar, is perched atop a large stone near the front entrance to the courthouse.

This Italianate super wedding-cake of a building is an architectural gem and is on the National Register of Historic Places.

Census: 1850—6,920 (Whites 6,450; Free Blacks 67; Slaves 403); **1950**—23,375; **1990**—51,043 (Whites 50,462; African Americans 216; Native Americans 130; Asians 203; Hispanics 237)

Per capita income (1991): $14,610; 76 percent of the national average

Land area: 592 square miles; drained by the French Broad River

Of interest: Appalachian Trail (a hiking trail from Georgia to Maine); Clingman's Dome, 6,643 feet; Dollywood Amusement Center; Douglas Lake; Foot Hills National Parkway; Gatlinburg ski resort and tourist center; Great Smoky Mountain National Park, 511,714 acres; Mt. LeConte, 6,593 feet.

Shelby County was established in 1819; named for Isaac Shelby who was active in the purchase of the Western District of Tennessee from the Chickasaw Nation. Memphis, named for the ancient city in Egypt, was founded by Andrew Jackson, Judge John Overton, and General James Winchester. The county seat of Shelby County was located in Memphis (1819–1827), in the town of Raleigh (1827–1867), and back in Memphis (1867–).

The first courthouse was built of logs on the public square in Memphis. In Raleigh there were two courthouses: a temporary frame building and, in 1864, a two-story brick building measuring 40 by 50 feet. Back in Memphis, the court met in a series of rented facilities until, in 1874, the bankrupt Overton Hotel was purchased and renovated for $150,000. By 1904 this building had become totally inadequate and the county was authorized to construct a building that would reflect the progressive nature of Shelby County. This present magnificent courthouse, costing approximately $1,600,000, was dedicated on January 1, 1910, and is on the National Register of Historic Places.

The Shelby County Courthouse was designed by the renowned New York architect, James Gamble Rogers; the principal contractors were John D. Pierce Company and Mathis Brothers Company. The exterior of the courthouse is of blue Bedford limestone; the interior makes use of marble from the four states of Tennessee, Alabama, Vermont, and Pennsylvania. Flanking the entrances are six heroic figures sculptured of white Tennessee marble representing Prosperity, Authority, Justice, Wisdom, Liberty, and Peace. Designed by J. Massey Rhind, these figures cost $74,302.10. The law library in the courthouse is renowned.

Over the years the courthouse suffered from exposure to the elements and lack of proper care. A modernization attempt in the 1960s proved unsuccessful. In 1983 the county embarked on a nine-year renovation project costing $18,600,000 which not only modernized the building but faithfully restored the courthouse to its original grandeur. The architectural firm was Design Associates and the general contractor, Inman Construction Company.

Census: 1850—31,157 (Whites 16,579; Free Blacks 218; Slaves 14,360); **1950**—482,393; **1990**—826,330 (Whites 455,063; African Americans 360,083; Native Americans 1,468; Asians 7,740; Hispanics 7,091)

Per capita income (1991): $19,200; 100 percent of the national average

Land area: 755 square miles; drained by the Mississippi River; Shelby County is the largest county in Tennessee in land area and in population

National Historic Landmark: Beale St. Historic District

Colleges: Christian Brothers University; Le Moyne-Owen College; Memphis College of Arts; Memphis State University; Rhodes College (formerly Southwestern College at Memphis); University of Tennessee at Memphis

Of interest: Children's Museum; Chucalissa Indian Village; Dixon Gallery and Gardens; Graceland (Home of Elvis Presley); Libertyland USA Amusement Park; Meeman-Shelby Forest State Park; Memphis Botanic Gardens; Memphis Brooks Museum of Art; Memphis Pink Palace Museum and Planetarium; Memphis Zoo; Mud Island and Mississippi River Museum; National Civil Rights Museum; National Ornamental Metal Museum; the Pyramid (coliseum and sports arena); Shelby Farms (largest urban park in the U.S.); T. O. Fuller State Park, Victorian Village; Edward Hull ("Boss Ed") Crump (–1954), politician; Richard Halliburton, (1900–1939) explorer and author; William Handy (1873–1958), "Father of the Blues"; Elvis Presley (1935–1977), "King of Rock and Roll." Governor Malcolm R. Patterson (1861–1935), Democrat, served 1907–1911; Governor Winfield Dunn (1927–), Republican, served 1971–1975; Governor Don Sundquist (1936–), Republican, (1995–), inaugurated governor in January 1995 in Nashville.

 *Smith County* was established in 1799; named in honor of Daniel Smith, colonel in the Revolutionary Army. Smith surveyed and made the first map of Tennessee, was secretary of the territory south of the River Ohio, and served as a senator from Tennessee, 1798–1799 and 1805–1809.

Carthage, named for the ancient Phoenician port in North Africa, was an active river port from the 1820s to the 1920s. Fleets of packets steamed the upper Cumberland River as far as Burnside, Kentucky. The steamboat trade was replaced by trucks when newly paved highways and bridges were completed.

The county seat was located on land belonging to Colonel William Walton, the builder of the famous "Walton Road" along which Walton built houses for the "entertainment" of travelers. The first court was held in the home of Tilman Dixon at Dixon Springs in 1799. The first courthouse was built in Carthage in 1805. The second, built in 1875 by E. P. Turner, architect, is still in use and is listed on the National Register of Historic Places.

Census: 1850—18,412 (Whites 13,709; Free Blacks 186; Slaves 4,517); **1950**—14,098; **1990**—14,143 (Whites 13,626; African Americans 459; Native Americans 36; Asians 13; Hispanics 48)

Per capita income (1991): $15,127; 79 percent of the national average

Land area: 314 square miles; drained by the Caney Fork and Cumberland Rivers

Of interest: Cordell Hull Lake and Dam; Old Hickory Lake. Governor Benton McMillin (1845–1933), Democrat, served 1899 to 1903. U.S. Senator Albert Gore Sr. and Vice President Albert Gore Jr. (1993–) have homes high on a hill overlooking Carthage.

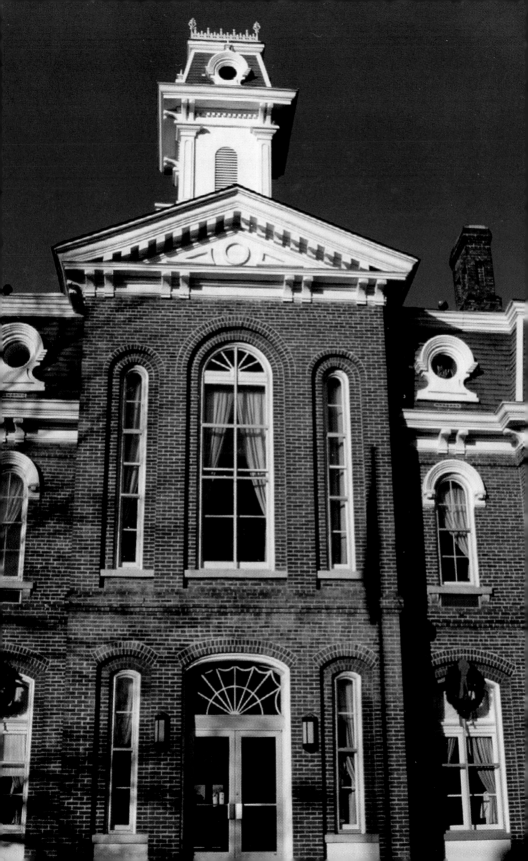

 ***Stewart County*** was established in 1803; named for Duncan Stewart, Revolutionary War veteran and early settler in the area. Dover was named by English settlers; the cliffs along the Cumberland River reminded them of the white cliffs of Dover.

Stewart County has had four courthouses: the first, built in 1806 for $600, was a one-story double-log building; the second, built in 1823 of brick, was destroyed by Federal troops in 1862; the third, built in 1870 for $14,000, was a square, two-story brick structure with tower. The present courthouse was erected in 1965 on land adjoining the square. Wilson & Odom were the architects.

Land Between the Lakes (Kentucky and Barkley Lakes), a popular recreational area, features a large herd of bison and "Homeplace 1850," a living history farm.

Census: 1850—9,719 (Whites 7,017; Free Blacks 127; Slaves 2,575); **1950**—9,175; **1990**—9,479 (Whites 9,294; African Americans 96; Native Americans 56; Asians 26; Hispanics 48)

Per capita income (1991): $12,244; 64 percent of the national average

Land area: 458 square miles; drained by the Cumberland and Tennessee Rivers

Of interest: Cross Creek National Wildlife Refuge; Fort Campbell; Fort Donelson National Military Park; Fort Henry site; nine historic iron furnaces dot the county.

Sullivan County was established

in 1779 (Tennessee's second oldest county); named for Major General John Sullivan, a distinguished officer in the Revolutionary War. The county seat was named for William Blount (see Blount County).

The first courthouse, a massive log structure built circa 1795, was used for 30 years until replaced by a brick courthouse in 1825. The third courthouse, built in 1853, was destroyed by fire with all the records in September 1863 during the Civil War. The walls remained intact, and the courthouse was restored in 1866. A fourth courthouse was built in 1895. The present courthouse, built in 1920, is on the National Register of Historic Places as part of the Blountville Historic District. Around it are many old buildings including, next door, the Old Deery Inn surrounded by large boxwoods. A new courthouse annex and criminal justice center with jail was completed at a new site in 1989.

Census: 1850—11,742 (Whites 10,603; Free Blacks 135; Slaves 1,004); **1950**—95,063; **1990**—143,596 (Whites 140,076; African Americans 2,562; Native Americans 372; Asians 485; Hispanics 521)

Per capita income (1991): $16,583; 87 percent of the national average

Land area: 413 square miles; drained by the Holston and headwaters of the Tennessee Rivers

National Historic Landmark: Long Island of the Holston

Of interest: Boone Lake; Bristol International Raceway; Cherokee National Forest; King College; Patrick Henry Lake; South Holston Lake; Warrior's Path State Recreational Park (1,342 acres). Governor John I. Cox (1857–1946), Democrat, served from 1905–1907.

Sumner County was established in 1786; named for Major General Jethro Sumner, veteran of the French and Indian War, the Revolutionary War, and the War of 1812. Gallatin was named for Albert Gallatin, secretary of the treasury under President Jefferson.

County court met in various places until 1802 when the land for Gallatin was purchased from James Trousdale. Sumner County has had three courthouses. The first, built in 1803, was a two-story building. The second, a brick building with a cupola topped with a round ball, was erected in 1839 and taken down in 1939. The present courthouse was completed in 1940 for an estimated $170,000. Marr & Holman of Nashville were the architects; W. R. Smith & Son of Nashville, the builders. A grant from the Federal Emergency Administration of Public Works of over $78,000 helped fund the courthouse. The courthouse was renovated in 1974–1975 and in 1993.

Census: 1850—22,717 (Whites 14,487; Free Blacks 224; Slaves 8,006); **1950**—33,533; **1990**—103,281 (Whites 97,073; African Americans 5,562; Native Americans 195; Asians 347; Hispanics 567)

Per capita income (1991): $17,313; 90 percent of the national average

Land area: 529 square miles; drained by the Cumberland River

National Landmarks: Wynnwood, Castalian Springs; Fairvue

Of interest: Cragfont, home of General James Winchester; Gallatin Presbyterian Church; Old Hickory Lake; Rock Castle. Governor William Hall (1775–1856), Democrat, served six months in 1829; Governor William Trousdale (1790–1872), Democrat, served 1849–1851; Governor William B. Campbell (1807–1867), Whig, served 1851–1853; Governor William B. Bate (1826–1905), Democrat, served 1883–1887.

 **Tipton County** was established in 1823; named for Jacob Tipton who was killed in 1791 during the defense of the Northwest Territory against the Indians. The county seat was named for General Leonard Wales Covington who died in 1813 at the Battle of Chrystlers Field.

Covington was established in 1825; the sale of 106 lots brought $8500 for use in setting up the town and building the public buildings. The first "temporary" courthouse, a small frame structure built in 1825 for $250, was demolished in 1831. The second, a two-story brick building constructed in 1832 by Darr Cox and William D. Walton, was extensively repaired in 1847 and in 1876. The present courthouse was built in 1889 for $24,500. McDonald Brothers were the architects; W. F. Boone the builder. In 1909 the courthouse tower was blown down by a tornado. The courthouse was remodeled in 1976–1977.

Census: 1850—8,887 (Whites 4,673; Free Blacks 22; Slaves 4,192); **1950**—29,782; **1980**—32,930; **1990**—37,568 (Whites 28,436; African Americans 8,852; Native Americans 114; Asians 100; Hispanics 253)

Per capita income (1991): $14,581; 76 percent of the national average

Land area: 459 square miles; bounded on the west by the Mississippi River; on the north by the Hatchie River

Of interest: Randolph, a town on the Mississippi promoted by David Crockett and bitter rival of Memphis, was burned during the Civil War.

 *Trousdale County* was established in 1870; named in honor of Governor William Trousdale who served with Andrew Jackson in the War of 1812, was a brigadier general in the Mexican War, served as governor of Tennessee from 1849–1851, and was later U.S. minister to Brazil. Hartsville was named for James Hart whose land was purchased for the town.

The first court was held in the Methodist church at Hartsville in 1870. The first courthouse, built in 1875 for $10,082.15 by Joe B. Patton, burned in 1900. The second courthouse, completed in December 1901, burned in August 1904. The third courthouse was barely completed in December 1904 when it burned with all the records. The 1905 courthouse is in use today and is on the National Register of Historic Places as part of the Hartsville Historic District. An obelisk in front of the courthouse commemorates the veterans of the wars of 1776, 1812, 1861, and 1898.

Census: 1880—6,646; 1950—5,520; 1990—5,920 (Whites 5,040; African Americans 853; Native Americans 14; Asians 8; Hispanics 31)

Per capita income (1991): $13,510; 70 percent of the national average

Land area: 114 square miles; the smallest county in Tennessee; drained by the Cumberland River

Of interest: The Battle of Hartsville was fought on December 7, 1862 when the Federal garrison, after one hour's fight, surrendered to the Confederates under General John Morgan. The construction of a nuclear power plant, nearing completion when Congress cut off funds, was abandoned in 1983.

Unicoi County was established in

1875. The name is from an Indian word, *u'nika*, said to mean "white, hazy, fog-draped." The Cherokee word has been variously spelled *u-ne-ga*, or *unika*, or *una-kaw*. The Tennessee legislature finally settled on *unicoi* as the spelling for the county.

The county seat was named Vanderbilt in 1876 in the hope of attracting Cornelius Vanderbilt to the area; however, he built his estate instead at Biltmore in western North Carolina. In 1879 the name changed to Ervin in honor of Dr. J. N. Ervin, an outstanding citizen of the area. Later the name was changed to Erwin in honor of Unicoi's first court clerk, Jesse B. Erwin. For a time the post office was named Erwin and the town Ervin, but Erwin prevailed.

The first court met at the Indian Creek Baptist Church in January 1876. The first courthouse, built in 1876–1877, was replaced in 1915. In 1976, the present courthouse was dedicated. Hart, Freeland & Roberts, were the architects; J. I. Cornett Construction Company, the builders; the cost, $1,097,393.22.

Census: 1880—3,645; 1950—15,886; 1990—16,549 (Whites 16,488; African Americans 3; Native Americans 11; Asians 14; Hispanics 97)

Per capita income (1991): $13,327; 69 percent of the national average

Land area: 186 square miles; drained by the Nolichucky River

Of interest: Big Bald Mountain (5,516 feet); Cherokee National Forest; Flint Creek Battle site where Colonel John Sevier battled Indians.

Following a performance of the Sparks Brothers Circus in Kingsport, Big Mary, billed as the largest elephant in captivity, ran amuck and killed her temporary trainer, Walter Eldridge; a trial was held and Big Mary was hanged from a railroad derrick in Erwin on September 12, 1917, before some 5000 witnesses.

 *Union County* was established in 1850. Two theories exist regarding the origin of its name. It was either the strong unionist sentiment of the people at the time of the Civil War, or the formation of the county by the union of parts of five counties (Anderson, Campbell, Claiborne, Grainger, Knox). The county seat was named in honor of Horace Maynard.

The organization of the county was delayed by a suit brought by the people of Knox County against forming Union County. In 1853 the suit was decided in favor of the county after Horace Maynard, a member of Congress, defended Union County. The first courts were held at Liberty Meeting House. The first brick courthouse was built in 1858. A second courthouse, built in 1900, burned in 1969. The present courthouse was built in 1974. Martin J. Lide was the architect; Mullins Construction Company, the contractor. Bronze plaques at the courthouse entrance honor country music

stars Chet Atkins, Carl Smith, and, the late "King of Country Music" Roy Acuff, all natives of the county.

Census: 1870—7,605; 1950—8,670; 1990—13,694 (Whites 13,658; African Americans 3; Native Americans 23; Asians 5, Hispanics 38)

Per capita income (1991): $10,291; 54 percent of the national average

Land area: 224 square miles; drained by the Clinch and Powell Rivers

Of interest: Big Ridge State Park (3,600 acres); Central Peninsula State Park; Norris Lake.

Van Buren County was established in 1840; named in honor of Martin Van Buren, eighth president of the United States 1837–1841. The county seat was named for Thomas Sharp "Big Foot" Spencer who was killed by Indians in the county.

Van Buren County has had three courthouses, all occupying successively the same one-acre, tree-shaded public square. The first was of hewn logs; the second, of brick, was used until 1906 when the county decided to build a new courthouse. Before the new building was completed, a tornado ripped through the town and lifted the roof from the courthouse, delaying construction. In recent years the building has been extensively renovated.

Census: 1850—2,674 (Whites 2,481; Free Blacks 18; Slaves 175); **1950**—3,985; **1990**—4,846 (Whites 4,823; African Americans 5; Native Americans 16; Asians 0; Hispanics 10)

Per capita income (1991): $9,719; 51 percent of the national average

Land area: 274 square miles; drained by the Caney Fork and Rocky Rivers

Of interest: Big Bone Cave State Park; Bledsoe State Forest. Fall Creek Falls State Resort Park, 16,000 acres, has the highest falls (256 feet) east of the Rockies.

Van Buren County Seat—Spencer, Tennessee 38585   113

Warren County was established in 1807; named for General Joseph Warren who was killed at the Battle of Bunker Hill in 1775. The county seat was named for Joseph McMinn (see McMinn County).

Early courts met at the home of Joseph Westmoreland and occasionally in a log house near Poplar Tavern. A log courthouse was built at Tanyard Springs. In 1810 McMinnville was chosen county seat. A brick courthouse with cupola was built in 1811 by Captain William White. In 1858 a brick courthouse was built for $12,000 by Goodney. The present 1897 courthouse is on the National Register of Historic Places. R. H. Hunt was the architect. B. M. Nelson was the builder; and Whitman & Stone, the stone contractor.

The area around McMinnville is famous for nurseries and orchards. The diversity of soil, climate, and elevation contributes to the development of a wide variety of agricultural products.

Census: 1850—10,179 (Whites 8,386; Free Blacks 83; Slaves 1,710); **1950**—22,271; **1990**—32,992 (Whites 31,511; African Americans 1,131; Native Americans 51; Asians 119; Hispanics 276)

Per capita income (1991): $12,939; 67 percent of the national average

Land area: 433 square miles; drained by the Collins and Barren Fork Rivers

Of interest: Center Hill Lake; Cumberland Caverns; Rock Island State Rustic Park.

Rumor has it that Judge Joshua Haskell, who presided over the Eighth District Court, was impeached in 1829 for going out behind the courthouse and eating a watermelon while a case was being tried in his court.

 **Washington County** was established in 1777 by the General Assembly of North Carolina before the state of Tennessee was formed; named for the first president George Washington. The state of Franklin (Frankland), formed in 1784, had Jonesborough as its capital and John Sevier as its first, and only, governor. Jonesborough, the oldest town in Tennessee, was established in 1799 and named for Willie Jones, a North Carolina politician friendly to the settlers beyond the mountains. In 1983 the spelling of the name was changed from *Jonesboro* back to the original Jonesborough.

Jonesborough has had seven courthouses. The records are intact from 1780. The first three courthouses were of logs and were built in 1778 by James Carter, in 1784 or 1785 by Charles Robertson, and in 1794. The third was a two-story structure with the jail located on the ground floor. The fourth courthouse, built of brick in 1820, burned in 1839. Rented quarters on Main Street served from 1839 to 1846 until the new courthouse was completed. The 1846 courthouse, costing $7000, had a dome and a clock which faced four directions. Jacob Newman of Knoxville and William Fleming of Jonesborough were the contractors. The clock cost an additional four hundred dollars. This courthouse was used as a hospital by the Confederate army during the Civil War.

The current courthouse was erected in 1912–1913. Bauman & Bauman were the architects; L. A. Galyon, the builder. The 1847 clock was installed in the new building and continues to give time to the community. In 1969 the Jonesborough Historic District, of which the courthouse is a part, was the first in Tennessee to be given a place on the National Register of Historic Places. At the entrance to the courthouse is a large bronze plaque inscribed with the Ten Commandments. Renovation in 1985 to the annex and in 1986–1987 to the courthouse cost approximately $110,663.52 and $1,757,548.31 respectively. The architect for both projects was Beeson, Lusk & Street; the contractor, Marshall Norman Construction Company.

Washington County now has two courthouses; one is in Jonesborough, the other in Johnson City. In 1935 the old post office in Johnson City was converted into the Ashe Street Courthouse. The Washington County Downtown Centre in Johnson City was built in 1986 and cost $2,385,047.12. The architect was Abernathy, Robinson & McGahey; the contractor, Jim Powell Construction Company.

Census: 1850—13,861 (Whites 12,671; Free Blacks 260; Slaves 930); **1950**—59,971; **1990**—92,315 (Whites 88,409; African Americans 3,275; Native Americans 155; Asians 378; Hispanics 471)

Per capita income: (1991) $16,664; 87 percent of the national average

Land area: 326 square miles; drained by the Nolichucky and the Watauga Rivers

Of interest: Boone Lake; Cherokee National Forest; East Tennessee State University; Jonesborough Days Celebration, July 4; National Storytelling (first weekend in October); Plum Grove archaeological site. Andrew Jackson was admitted to the bar in Jonesborough.

Wayne County

was established in 1819; named for Major General Anthony Wayne of the Revolutionary army. His daring exploits, usually successful, earned him the nickname "Mad Anthony." The first county seat was at "Old Town" at Tom Branch, four miles north of Waynesboro, where a log courthouse was built. The county seat moved to Waynesboro in 1822.

A log courthouse was built and used until 1827 when it was replaced by a frame courthouse. In 1843–1844 a substantial brick courthouse was built for $5000. Nathan Thomas of Franklin was the architect; D. G. Grimes and John A. Talley, the builders. In 1905 a concrete-block courthouse, with stone trim, cupola and clock, was constructed for approximately $25,000. Designed by W. Chamberlin & Company, this courthouse was destroyed by fire in 1973. In 1975 a fireproof courthouse, costing $1,000,000 and described as "a space age courthouse in a Civil War setting," was built of reinforced concrete with marble trim. Yearwood & Johnson of Nashville were the architects; W. C. Moore Construction Company of Waynesboro, the builder.

Census: 1850—8,170 (Whites 7,232; Free Blacks 8; Slaves 930); 1950—13,863; 1990—13,935 (Whites 13,762; African Americans 137; Native Americans 17; Asians 10; Hispanics 52)

Per capita income (1991): $11,788; 61 percent of the national average

Land area: 734 square miles; drained by the Tennessee and Buffalo Rivers

Of interest: Natchez Trace State Parkway, 43,000 acres. Natural Bridge, an impressive double-span natural stone bridge located at Rainbow Lake on "Forty-eight Branch in Court House Hollow" off the Buffalo River, was used by the Indians as a council ground and camping area; it also served as the "Stone Courthouse" where, in the early days, circuit courts were held for Hardin and Wayne Counties; a horse thief was said to have once been tried, sentenced, and hung on the spot. The area was also a favorite hideout for bandits who preyed on travelers on the Natchez Trace.

 **Weakley County** was established in 1823; named for Robert Weakley, prominent early pioneer. Dresden was named for Dresden, Germany, the birthplace of the father of a commissioner who laid out the town.

Weakley County has had three courthouses. The first, a brick building forty feet square, was built by John Scarborough of Stewart County. The second, a two-story brick courthouse built in the 1850s by Major Cowardin for $20,000, was enlarged and renovated in 1911, and burned in 1948. The present courthouse, built in 1948–1950 for $720,000, is finished with Alabama limestone. Marr & Holman of Nashville were the architects; Seth E. Giem & Associates of Memphis, the contractors.

Census: 1850—14,608 (Whites 11,525; Free Blacks 13; Slaves 3,070); **1950**—27,962; **1990**—31,972 (Whites 29,368; African Americans 2,222; Native Americans 39; Asians 277; Hispanics 128)

Per capita income (1991): $13,882; 72 percent of the national average

Land area: 580 square miles; drained by the Obion River

Of interest: Big Cypress Tree State Park; University of Tennessee at Martin. Governor Ned Ray McWherter (1930–), Democrat, served 1987–1994.

 **White County** was established in 1806; named in honor of John White, veteran of the Revolutionary War and an early settler in the area. Sparta was established as the county seat in 1809 and named for the ancient Greek city.

White County has had four court-houses. The first, of logs, was used from 1810–1815; the second, of brick, served from 1815–1894. The 1894 courthouse, a large brick structure, was demolished in 1974 to make way for the courthouse completed in 1975 at the cost of $1,000,000. Marton J. Lide of Birmingham was the architect; Hardaway Construction Company of Nashville, the builders. The courthouse was dedicated at a gala ceremony in November 1975. U.S. Congressman Joe L. Evins, representative from the Fourth District since 1946, was the speaker and a signer of the "Second Declaration of Independence" prepared for the occasion.

Census: 1850—11,444 (Whites 10,101; Free Blacks 129; Slaves 1,214); **1950**—16,204; **1990**—20,090 (Whites 19,654; African Americans 378; Native Americans 24; Asians 25; Hispanics 74)

Per capita income (1991): $12,949; 68 percent of the national average

Land area: 377 square miles; drained by Caney Fork River

Of interest: Burgess Falls State Natural Area (also in Putnam County); Center Hill Lake; Rock Island State Rustic Park (also in Warren County); Virgin Falls State Natural Area.

Williamson County was established in 1799; named for Dr. Hugh Williamson, surgeon general of the North Carolina Militia during the Revolution and member of the Continental Congress. The county seat was named for Benjamin Franklin.

Williamson County has had three courthouses. The first two courthouses were located in the center of the square: the first built of logs in 1800; the second of brick in 1809. The present antebellum courthouse, built in 1859 at a cost of approximately $20,000, stands facing the square. John W. Miller was in charge of construction; iron for the columns, cast in a foundry in Franklin, was strip-mined along the Caney Fork Creek; the brick walls are 24 inches thick; the foundation is made of huge dressed stones quarried in the Carter's Creek area; the doors are of quarter-inch sheets of wrought iron. For years the courthouse bricks were painted white but, in 1976, extensive renovations costing some $770,000 included sandblasting to restore the original bricks and the construction of an addition similar in size and style to the original building. Richard C. Williams was the architect; Ralph E. Koch, the contractor. The Confederate monument and cannon remain in the town square. The courthouse is in the Franklin Historic District on the National Register of Historic Places.

Census: 1850—27,201 (Whites 14,266; Free Blacks 71; Slaves 12,861); **1950**—25,220; **1990**—81,021 (Whites 74,903; African Americans 5,396; Native Americans 130; Asians 469; Hispanics 522)

Per capita income (1991): $25,089; 131 percent of the national average

Land area: 582 square miles; drained by the Harpeth River

National Historic Landmarks: Franklin Battlefield (reenacted yearly); Hiram Johnson Masonic Lodge No. 7

Of Interest: Battle Ground Academy; Carter House; Confederate Cemetery Lane; Carnton Mansion; Crow Cut Road; Fort Grainger; Liberty Hill School; Natchez Trace Parkway (see Hickman County). Future generations may marvel at the magnificent double-arched bridge of the Natchez Trace Parkway that sails across a valley over Highway 96 near the borders of Davidson and Williamson Counties; the pyramids of ancient Egypt might comfortably rest beneath the arches, but alas, the mind-expanding bridge is set in a remote place, only fully appreciated from a trip down Highway 96 off of Highway 100 near the end of the Trace. Governor Newton Cannon (1781–1841), Whig, served 1835–1839; Governor John Price Buchanan (1847–1930), Democrat, served 1891–1893.

 **Wilson County** was established in 1799; named for David Wilson who served in the Revolutionary War, in the Territorial Assembly, and as speaker of the state house of representatives. The county seat was named for the biblical Lebanon because of the many cedar trees in the area.

Wilson County has had five courthouses. The first, of cedar logs, was built circa 1806. The second, built in 1811, was graced by a cupola, bell, and gilded eagle. The third courthouse, built in 1848 and designed by William Strickland, architect, burned in 1881. The fourth courthouse was built in 1882–1884 at a cost of $17,000. Smith & Rome were the architects; J. F. Bowers & Brothers, builders. The present courthouse, costing $935,465, was built in 1966 on East Main Street (the land cost $150,735). The architects were Morton-Carter Associates of Nashville; the builder, Richard E. Hunt of Lebanon. The monument of Confederate General Robert Hatton stands watch over the original courthouse square.

Census: 1850—27,443 (Whites 19,913; Free Blacks 403; Slaves 7,127); **1950**—26,315; **1990**—67,675 (Whites 62,561; African Americans 4,607; Native Americans 185; Asians 259; Hispanics 386)

Per capita income (1991): $17,390; 91 percent of the national average

Land area: 571 square miles; drained by the Cumberland River

Of interest: Cedars of Lebanon State Recreational Park; Cumberland University; Old Hickory Lake; Sam Houston's Law Office; Sellars Indian Mound. Governor James C. "Lean Jimmy" Jones (1809–1859), Whig, served 1841–1845.

Bibliography

Alderman, Pat. *Greasy Cove in Unicoi County*. The Overmountain Press, 1975.

Barry, William L. "A Note on Henderson County." *Tennessee Historical Quarterly*, Spring, 1975.

Beach, Ursula S. *Montgomery County*. Tennessee County History Series, Memphis: Memphis State University Press, 1988.

Beasley, Gaylon N. *True Tales of Tipton*. Covington: The Tipton County Historical Society, 1981.

Blankenship, Harold C. *History of Macon County, Tennessee*. Tompkinsville: Monroe County Press, 1986.

Bowman, Virginia M. *Historic Williamson County*. Nashville: Blue & Grey Press, 1971.

Brandt, Robert. *Touring the Middle Tennessee Backroads*. Winston-Salem: John F. Blair, 1995.

Brazelton, B. G. *A History of Hardin County*. Cumberland Presbyterian Publishing House, 1885.

Bridgewater, Betty Anderson. "A Look at Coffee County Courthouse." *Coffee County Historical Quarterly*, Winter, 1971.

Brookes, R., M.D. *General Gazetteer*. Philadelphia: Johnson & Warner, 1812.

Brown, Sterling S. *History of Woodbury and Cannon County, Tennessee*. Manchester: Doak Printing Co., 1936.

Burns, G. Frank. *Davidson County*. Tennessee County History Series, Memphis: Memphis State University Press, 1989.

————. *Wilson County*. Tennessee County History Series, Memphis: Memphis State University Press, 1983.

Burns, Inez E. *History of Blount County, 1795–1955*. Mary Blount Chapter, DAR, Tennessee Historical Commission, 1957.

Burt, Eleanor B. J. "A Note on Jefferson County." *Tennessee Historical Quarterly*, Summer, 1974.

Byrum, C. Stephen. *McMinn County*. Tennessee County History Series, Memphis: Memphis State University Press, 1984.

Camp, Henry R. *Sequatchie County*. Tennessee County History Series, Memphis: Memphis State University Press, 1984.

Campbell, T. J. *Records of Rhea, A Condensed County History.* Dayton: Rhea Publishing Co., 1940, reproduced 1976.

Clayton, W. W. *History of Davidson County, Tennessee.* Philadelphia, Penn., 1880.

Cohen, Nelle Roller. "Pulaski History." *Pulaski Citizen,* 1948–1950, published 1951.

Cowlew, Robert E. *A History of Dickson County.* The Tennessee Historical Commission & The Dickson County Historical Society, Nashville, Tenn., 1956.

Dickinson, W. Calvin. *Morgan County.* Tennessee County History Series, Memphis: Memphis State University Press, 1987.

Dykeman, Wilma. *Tennessee, a Bicentennial History.* New York: W. W. Norton & Company, Inc., 1975.

Ethridge, Robert L. and Mary T. *Bicentennial Echoes of the History of Overton County.* Livingston: Enterprise Printing Co., 1976.

Ewell, Gerald L. "A Note on Coffee County." *Tennessee Historical Quarterly,* Winter, 1974.

Federal Writers Project, W.P.A. *Tennessee, A Guide to the State.* American Guide Series, New York: Hastings House, 1939.

Fink, Paul M. *Jonesborough: The First Century of Tennessee's First Town.* Nashville, Tenn., 1972.

Foster, A. P. *Counties of Tennessee.* Nashville, Tenn., 1923.

Goodspeed, W. A., et al., eds. *History of Tennessee.* Nashville, Tenn., 1887.

Hale, Will T. *Early History of Warren County.* McMinnville: Standard Printing Company, 1930.

Harper, Herbert L. "The Antebellum Courthouses of Tennessee." *Tennessee Historical Quarterly,* Spring, 1971.

Hendrickson, Mrs. T. J. *A Short History of Sumner County, 1786–1957.* Sumner County Library Board, 1957.

Holt, Edgar. *Claiborne County.* Tennessee County History Series, Memphis: Memphis State University Press, 1981.

Hoskins, Katherine B. *Anderson County.* Tennessee County History Series, Memphis: Memphis State University Press, 1979.

Huddleston, Tim. *History of Pickett County, Tennessee.* Collegedale: The College Press, 1973.

Killebrew, J. B. *Introduction to the Resources of Tennessee.* Nashville, Tenn., 1874.

Krechniak, Helen B., & J. M. *Cumberland County's First Hundred Years.* Centennial Committee, Crossville, Tenn., 1956.

Layne, Mrs. Ora. *Sequatchie County.* Dunlap, Tenn., 1969.

Lillard, Roy G. *Bradley County.* Tennessee County History Series, Memphis: Memphis State University Press, 1980.

Lillard, Stewart. *Meigs County, Tennessee.* Cleveland: The Book Shelf, 1975, revised 1982.

Link, G. B. *A History of Marion County.* Paper for Master's Degree, 1953.

Livingood, James W. *Hamilton County.* Tennessee County History Series, Memphis: Memphis State University Press, 1981.

Map Guide to the U.S. Federal Census, 1790–1920. Baltimore: Genealogical Publishing Company, Inc., 1987.

Marshall, E. H., *History of Obion County.* Reprinted by Union City: H. A. Lazer Co., 1970.

Mason, Robert L. *Cannon County*. Tennessee County History Series, Memphis: Memphis State University Press, 1982.

McBride, Robert M. "The Lost Counties of Tennessee." The East Tennessee Historical Society's Publications, no. 38, 1966.

McClain, Ira Hopkins. *A History of Houston County*. Published by the author, 1966.

———. *A History of Stewart County*. Published by the author, 1966.

McMurty, J. C. *History of Trousdale County*. Vidett Publishing Co., 1970.

McPeak, Patricia L. S. "A Note on Monroe County." *Tennessee Historical Quarterly*, Fall, 1975.

Mercer, Theodore, C. "A Note on Rhea County." *Tennessee Historical Quarterly*, Spring, 1976.

Merritt, Frank. *Early History of Carter County, 1760–1861*. East Tennessee Historical Society, Knoxville, Tenn., 1950.

———. *Later History of Carter County, 1865–1980*. Heritage Project, Elizabethton, Tenn., 1986.

Morris, Eastin. *Tennessee Gazetteer 1834*. Reprint edited by Robert M. McBride and Owen Meredith, Nashville: The Gazetteer Press, 1971.

Morrison Jr., J. F. *A Brief History of Early Lawrence County, Tennessee*. Published by the county historian, 1968.

Nicholson, James L. *Grundy County*. Tennessee County History Series, Memphis: Memphis State University Press, 1982.

Page, Bonnie, M. *Anderson County: Its Cities, Towns and Points of Interest*. Published by the author, Lake City, Tenn., 1986.

———. *Campbell County*. Published by the author, Lake City, Tenn., 1986.

———. *Claiborne County*. Published by the author, Lake City, Tenn., 1986.

———. *Union County*. Published by the author, Lake City, Tenn., 1986.

Peters, Kate J., ed. *Lauderdale County from Earliest Times*. Sugar Hill Lauderdale County Library, Ripley, Tenn., 1957.

Pittard, Mabel B. *Rutherford County*. Tennessee County History Series, Memphis: Memphis State University Press, 1984.

Puetz, C. J. *Tennessee County Maps*. County Maps, Lyndon Station: Puetz Place.

Putnam, A. W. *History of Middle Tennessee: The Life and Times of James Robertson*. Nashville, Tenn., 1859.

Raulston, J. L. & J. W. Livingood. *Sequatchie*. Knoxville: University of Tennessee Press, 1974.

Rhoton, T. F. *A Brief History of Franklin County, Tennessee*. Published by the author, 1941, reprint 1966.

Roddy, Vernon. "A Note on Macon County." *Tennessee Historical Quarterly*, Fall, 1974.

Rothrock, Mary V., ed. *The French Broad-Holston Country, A History of Knox County*. Knox County Historical Commission, East Tennessee Historical Society, 1946.

Russell, Janette C. *The Shelby County Court: Renovation and Restoration, 1980–1992*. Shelby County Government, Memphis, Tenn., 1994.

Sakowski, Carolyn. *Touring the East Tennessee Backroads*. Winston-Salem: John F. Blair, 1993.

Sanderson, Ester Sharp. *County Scott and Its Mountain Folk*. Published by the author, Huntsville, Tenn., 1978.

Sands, Sarah G. Cox. *History of Monroe County, Tennessee.* Baltimore: Gateway Press, Inc., 1982.

Shelby County Commemorative. *The Courthouse: Shelby County, Tennessee, 1909–1984.* Memphis, Tenn., 1984.

Siler, Tom. *Tennessee Towns: from Adams to Yorkville.* East Tennessee Historical Society, Knoxville, Tenn., 1985.

Smith, Jonathan K. *Benton County.* Tennessee County History Series, Memphis: Memphis State University Press, 1979.

Smith, Reid. *Majestic Middle Tennessee.* Prattville: Paddle Wheel Publications, 1975.

Stewart, G. Tillman. *Henderson County.* Tennessee County History Series, Memphis: Memphis State University Press, 1979.

Taylor, Oliver. *Historic Sullivan, A History of Sullivan County, Tennessee.* Bristol: The King Printing Co., 1909.

Tennessee Department of Economic & Community Development Reports. *Economic Indicators,* 1994; *Tennessee Population by County and Place by Race,* 1990.

Tennessee Historical Commission. *Tennessee Historical Markers,* 1972.

Tennessee Secretary of State. *Tennessee Blue Book,* 1975–1976, 1987–1988, 1991–1994.

Thorndale, William & William Dollarhide. *Map Guide to the U.S. Federal Censuses, 1790–1820.* Baltimore: Genealogical Publishing Co., Inc., 1987.

Vaughan, Virginia C. *Weakley County.* Tennessee County History Series, Memphis: Memphis State University Press, 1983.

Wear, Jerry L. *Sevierville, 1795–1986.* Sevierville Heritage Committee, 1986.

Webb, Thomas G. *DeKalb County.* Tennessee County History Series, Memphis: Memphis State University Press, 1986

Wells, Ann Harwell. "Checklist of Tennessee Maps, 1820–1830." *Tennessee Historical Quarterly,* Fall, 1984.

Williams, Emma Inman. *Historic Madison.* Madison County Historical Society, 1946.

Wingfield, Marshall. "Tipton County, Tennessee." West Tennessee Historical Papers, no. 3, 1949.

Womack, Walter. *McMinnville at a Milestone.* Published by author, McMinnville, Tenn., 1960.

Wooten, J. M. *A History of Bradley County.* Bradley County Post #81, The American Legion/Tennessee Historical Commission, 1949.

Younger, Lillye. *Decatur County.* Tennessee County History Series, Memphis: Memphis State University Press, 1979.

Index